The American Civil War

An Enthralling Overview of the War Between States

Free limited time bonus

Stop for a moment. We have a free bonus set up for you. The problem is this: we forget 90% of everything that we read after 7 days. Crazy fact, right? Here's the solution: we've created a printable, 1-page pdf summary for this book that you're reading now. All you have to do to get your free pdf summary is to go to the following website: **https://livetolearn.lpages.co/enthrallinghistory/**

Once you do, it will be intuitive. Enjoy, and thank you!

Table of Contents

Introduction

The American Civil War has become one of the most defining moments in US history. Not a century had passed since the Declaration of Independence, which was adopted in July 1776. Since gaining independence and existing as a sovereign nation, complex social, political, and economic issues had been quietly growing in the United States. Instead of addressing them, the country was distracted by different priorities, mainly acquiring new territories and becoming a regional superpower. However, by the 1860s, the divide within American society reached its peak. The nation disintegrated into four years of bloody conflicts and instability, which cost the lives of more than one million Americans.

Compared to other major US conflicts, the Civil War holds a special place in the hearts of Americans. The war was a pivotal point in the 19th century and completely changed the course of the country. The consequences of the Civil War can still be felt today, as the country is perhaps the most polarized it has been for a very long time. Some compare it to the infamous North-South divide. Despite the immense importance of the war for the US and, to a large extent, world history, many people outside the US are unfamiliar with what happened almost 160 years ago.

This book wishes to cover the extremely interesting history of the American Civil War and explain the events that took place. Not only will the book provide an overview of the main events that shaped the American Civil War, but it will also explore many details that are often left out when discussing the conflict.

The first part of the book will be devoted to the situation that existed in the United States before the start of the war in 1861. It will cover the events that led to the extreme socio-political turmoil of the country by the end of the 1850s and talk about some of the main differences between the Northern and Southern states. It will also discuss the extremely important concept of Manifest Destiny and how it impacted the growth of America for the first part of the 19th century. Then, we will turn our attention to the Mexican-American War, the Texas question, and the effects these events had on slavery. Finally, we will talk about the political processes in the 1850s, which escalated the tensions between the Northern and the Southern states, and explore the severity of the divide within the country.

The middle part of the book covers the actual conflict itself. Explore the chronological account of the war, and learn about the figures who made a name for themselves. The book will also cover all of the theaters of the war in great detail, starting from the Eastern and Western Fronts in the heart of the United States to the Trans-Mississippi, Pacific, and Lower Seaboard theaters near the Gulf of Mexico. The American Civil War remains the largest conflict fought in the US. Diving into details about the campaigns is pivotal in understanding how the war unfolded over the years.

Finally, the book will talk about the outcome of the war and its end. We will explain the circumstances that led to the North's victory over the South and the final stages of the conflict. Then, discover the immediate and long-term consequences of the Civil War. We will also mention the international reaction that followed the end of the conflict. Examining these effects is crucial in understanding the influence the war had on the US and the rest of the free world.

The American Civil War is perceived to be a conflict where the side that fought for the values of freedom, democracy, and social equality managed to emerge victorious. Besides being a pivotal point in US history, it also is one of the most popular ideological clashes in the 19th century. To some degree, the war was inevitable—one could see the tensions between the two sides from a mile away—but this factor, coupled with many other reasons, is why this war holds a special place in the hearts of Americans. So, let's dive into the American Civil War, one of the most instantly recognizable conflicts in history.

Chapter 1 – 19th-Century America

Let's take a look at some of the existing issues in the American socio-political landscape, from the early 19th century all the way to the 1850s—the decade that preceded the American Civil War. We will focus mainly on the ideological struggle present in the country at the beginning of the 1800s, as well as describe the general economic structure of the US. Historians often disagree on which of these issues is the true "cause" of the Civil War. However, instead of focusing on individual issues, it is better to provide a general overview of the situation that existed prior to the start of the war.

The Land of the Free and the Different

As many historians have recognized, the United States in the 19th century was differently organized than other countries in the world, something that was even noticed by the European contemporaries who visited the States back then. Europe had essentially given birth to America and American society, but the US was not modeled after the European states. The pro-democratic movements in the late-18th-century US started a wave of nationalist revolutions throughout Europe, which characterized the continent for the whole of the 19th century.

This weird symbiotic relationship existed between the Old and New World, but it was only present in the US and not in other colonial or post-colonial European societies like, for example, Canada and Mexico. The United States was still being forged, both culturally and socially, by the time the Civil War began in the 1860s. It was also making developments in its unique political structures that largely defined the country since it gained independence in 1776. American society borrowed a lot from European societies, but whatever it borrowed, it tried to change in its own way.

In the 19th century, the country was still trying to find its footing in the world. The United States had been born under special circumstances. After centuries of colonization and outside rule, anti-imperialism was innate in the hearts of the average American. Their hatred toward Great Britain and King George united the American public, for the most part, during the Revolutionary War.

This anti-imperialist sentiment led to the promotion of freedom and liberty. However, it became clear that anti-imperialism could not be the only factor that glued American society together. Thus, most of the early 19th century was devoted to forging a new, unique American identity that would take the liberal democratic principles that the country had been founded upon and mix them with core European values to create something distinctive. Thanks to an array of factors, including rapid technological improvements, the age of industrialization, and geographic isolation, the Americans were able to get to work.

Practically every inch of Europe had been explored in great detail. The same could not be said about North America. Although the lands of the continent had been divided between the French, the Spanish, and the British, by the late 1810s, only the latter had any ambition, let alone the resources, to put up a challenge for North America. Europe had been swept up in a universal uproar due to Napoleon's conquests, which meant that both France and Spain had to mobilize the majority of their resources domestically, leaving their overseas possessions unattended. In turn, this caused the French to sell their North American territories—more than 828,000 square miles of land—in the famous Louisiana Purchase of 1807 to the ambitious United States. The Mexican Revolution effectively kicked the Spanish out of continental America by 1820.

The weakening of America's direct rivals meant there was an opening for the United States to sweep the continent and claim whatever it could for itself. The dream of stretching the American lands from the East Coast of the Atlantic to the West Coast of the Pacific was born. This idea became a defining characteristic of 19th-century American foreign policy. Manifest Destiny was imprinted into the minds of the Americans. It was a belief that the United States was destined by God to spread American ideals from the east to the west.

Inspired by this "righteous" idea, the American settlers swarmed the continent to try and expand American territories as far as they could, first colonizing the center of the continent before reaching the distant rich lands of California and Oregon. The settlers were resilient in their divine mission of spreading American ideas of liberty, democracy, and prosperity while claiming an immense chunk of land for themselves at the same time. They persisted despite the resistance they found, forcibly displacing natives. They were even ready to challenge the British over what they believed was rightfully theirs.

American Progress, a painting depicting the concept of Manifest Destiny.
https://commons.wikimedia.org/wiki/File:American Progress (John Gast painting).jpg

Thus, the idea of Manifest Destiny, in a way, was a diversion from anti-imperialism. Arguably, it was one of the earliest signs of American imperialism, as it displayed the qualities found in all empires of the 19th century, such as forced colonization and the spread of ideas. However, for the United States, Manifest Destiny was merely the fulfillment of its destiny, so its morality was rarely questioned. Most people paid attention to the spread of liberal, democratic principles instead of the ugly stuff.

Anti-imperialism was replaced by a form of anti-Europeanism, which is most clearly identified in the famous Monroe Doctrine of 1823. This was a policy by US President James Monroe that stated the United States would oppose the formation of any future European colonies in the Western Hemisphere. In exchange, it would remain neutral in European matters. The Monroe Doctrine fused with the concept of Manifest Destiny: the latter was a belief that the US was destined to colonize the rest of the continent by itself, while the former guaranteed that the US would be the only one that could do it. Both reflected the public sentiment of the time relatively well and promised a bright future. In addition, they also underlined the fact that the United States, although still a relatively new country, was ambitious and ready to stand up for itself, something that put it on the radar of the bigger European powers.

Even before the concepts of Manifest Destiny and the Monroe Doctrine became official, the country made an impressive effort to establish itself as a regional power. The War of 1812 was the first sign that signaled the United States was a force to be reckoned with, as the Americans withstood the mighty British forces and diminished Spain's influence in Spanish Florida. Although the Americans were not officially victorious in the war, they had clearly demonstrated they were powerful. After that, the United States was not afraid to challenge Britain over territorial disputes. Even though their rivalry never resulted in a war, the US managed to achieve several favorable outcomes.

One of the best examples of 19th-century American expansionism is the Mexican-American War, which ended in a decisive US victory. Mexico was forced to give up immense territorial concessions—about one-third of its territory. The war started over the issue of Texas, a province that had seceded from Mexico and wished to join the United States as a new state. The Americans easily overpowered the newly formed Mexican republic, which was plagued with domestic issues and an inferior military. As a result, the United States gained almost all of the modern Southwest, including the rich territories of California and Texas. By the end of the war, the United States had, in a way, fulfilled its destiny, as it occupied the heart of the North American continent from the East Coast all the way to the Pacific Ocean.

Thus, the first part of the 19th century was a productive period for US foreign policy. Since the early 1800s, the United States had developed its national identity around the ideas of continental expansion and anti-Europeanism. Let's look at how its assets allowed the US to cement its position as a regional powerhouse.

The 19th-century US Economy

As the decades passed after gaining independence, it became clearer that America's isolated geographic position was paying off. Its advantageous location, far away from the power centers of major European countries, meant the United States was relatively secure from external threats. The people's efforts and resources did not have to be used on countries challenging its growing power and influence. Thus, it should come as no surprise that the US economy, at least in the first part of the 19th century, grew far quicker than some may have predicted. The security provided by geographic isolation, paired with a motivated population to explore and colonize the unknown wilderness of the American continent, meant there was much for the taking with very little resistance from Europe.

Naturally, with such a massive landscape to claim, an important economic aspect showed itself early in the 19th century: the profit that could be made from deforestation. This was seen as a sort of win-win situation for the American settlers. They needed lands to settle on and set up agricultural or industrial bases, so huge chunks of land had to be deforested to make room for expansion. This meant that the country, in addition to its already vast coal and iron reserves, had a huge abundance of wood and timber—materials that could be used for energy, manufacturing, and an array of other useful things. Contrary to Europe, where wood was slowly starting to become a luxury due to increased levels of deforestation (a natural consequence of industrialization), the United States had the ability to not only freely use the timber it produced domestically but also have a significant amount left for export.

America's natural resources promised a bright future for the economy. At the beginning of the 1800s, the US still depended on the Old World, mainly Britain, which remained America's largest trading partner for decades. However, this factor could have been attributed to Britain starting the Industrial Revolution, as it gave the empire a natural head-start compared to its rivals. Industrialization in America followed soon after, despite the fact that the majority of the population lived in rural areas—something that was a consequence of dwelling in a largely unexplored continent. In the southern part of the country, the rural population outnumbered those who lived in urban areas. On the other hand, this meant cities easily sprung up in the new territories. Meanwhile, on the East Coast, New York, Philadelphia, and Boston dominated the scene. The American Midwest soon started to rise into prominence, with cities like Chicago and Cincinnati growing almost exponentially before the start of the Civil War.

A population boom further boosted economic growth. This boom was partially caused by a large number of immigrants who arrived in the US from Europe. They sought a new life, one that promised significant improvements from their old one. The country's population reached about twenty-five million in the 1850s; there had been only five million people at the start of the century. This was a promising improvement. All sorts of people were welcome to the country despite their age or profession. Many aspects of life were still in development, and everybody could do whatever fit them best.

An influx of people meant that it was very cheap to buy land, which was in abundance. The government had correctly recognized that the public lands in its possession would be put to better use in the hands of the American people. They sold an acre for $2 to not only the citizens of the country but also the immigrants. This was one of the biggest motivating factors for people to venture out west and settle there permanently. Although Native Americans already lived on the land, the open frontier was likely a somewhat welcome relief to the cramped conditions in the east. By the 1860s, the US government had sold about eighty million acres of land. The people who moved west were happy to develop their possessions as they liked with little regulations. The American Midwest rapidly grew in this period.

In short, the American economy never stopped growing after it achieved independence in 1776. Thanks to an array of factors, such as an abundance of land and resources, a sizeable workforce, and favorable conditions, the US economy quickly picked up the pace and started to catch up with its competitors in Europe. However, there is one vital detail we have not yet talked about: the role of slavery.

The Economics of Slavery

Slaves were pivotal not only to the structure of the American economy in the 19th century but also to many socio-political matters. We shall now look at the economic implications of slavery.

Since the age of colonization, slavery greatly helped the European colonizers in developing and maintaining their newly acquired territories. It was innate that with a blend of cultures, ethnicities, and religions, new hierarchical structures would form. In the colonies, slavery was just one part of the hierarchy, but it was not unknown to the dwellers of the Old World. After all, slaves had always been the lowest strata in every civilized society. They were often not even considered as people or citizens but rather as possessions or property. In the New World, slaves were seen in a similar light. They were used in agriculture, mining, industries, construction, and many other forms of labor.

A family of slaves in Georgia.
https://commons.wikimedia.org/wiki/File:Family_of_slaves_in_Georgia,_circa_1850.jpg

It is sometimes difficult to grasp the extent to which slavery existed in the US, as it was considered old-fashioned in other countries by the time the Civil War broke out. Because slavery was such an efficient way of generating income, it was considered one of the pillars of the American economy. This was more apparent in the Southern part of the country, which was far more dependent on slavery than the North. The Southern states thrived on agriculture, and they made a lot of money from their vast plantations, which were operated by the very slaves they owned. As the early 1800s started, it was clearer than ever that slave ownership was perhaps the most important aspect of the Southerners' lifestyle. It not only determined the wealth of the owners but also their status in society. The more slaves one owned, the more power one had.

The slaves lived in terrible conditions. They were abused and separated from their families time and time again. However, slaves dominated the population of some Southern states. Along the Mississippi River, in Alabama and Mississippi, as well as in South Carolina and parts of Virginia, they made up most of the population, making up about half of the whole population of the South. Thus, it should come as no surprise that the South was very reliant on slaves. Owning more slaves meant working more land, which, in turn, meant more direct income. Most of the country's agriculture, both domestically and in terms of foreign exports, originated in the South. With these funds, the Southern slave owners would try to expand their wealth by investing more. They would buy new territories and acquire new slaves to work their property.

It was a vicious cycle and a profitable endeavor with a great return on investment. It is important to keep in mind that with the concept of Manifest Destiny becoming more and more prevalent, Southern slave owners were more adamant about claiming new lands for themselves. Not only that, but rich slave owners, those who owned about a hundred slaves or more, lived probably the most lavishly in the whole country. Their properties spanned tens of acres. They had luxurious mansions, diverse plantations and farms, and nothing in the world to worry about. In turn, this motivated farmers who did not enjoy the same privileges to strive to attain the same lifestyle.

In the early 19th century, the South's prosperous slave economy put it in competition with the North, which was slowly abandoning slave ownership and its reliance on agriculture as a whole. Instead, its focus was on other industries, such as textile or machinery manufacturing. By the 1850s, the Southern slave owners had reached the peak of their wealth. In addition to making fortunes by selling and buying slaves, the market price of their products, especially cotton, increased almost exponentially during that period. The southerners, at least the ones at the top of the social stratum, could yield amazing results on their capital investments. They then spent their money on more luxurious and foreign products.

The Southern countryside was an impressive sight, with massive territories owned by single families and tens of slaves working their lands. Interestingly, many Southern planters became so rich from their endeavors that they no longer needed to live on their properties. Instead, they could move to more urban areas, which were popping up all over the country. They could move to the newly acquired lands out west or even leave America to enjoy lavish lives in Europe.

These were only some of the main characteristics of the early 19th-century United States. Since the beginning of the century, a new national identity based on expansion had gained a lot of traction. Supported by an anti-imperialist (or rather an anti-European) foreign policy, the United States saw itself as the sole "protector" of the Western Hemisphere from the old systems of the tyrannical Europeans. All of this generated a drive in the public to acquire and modernize more territories, which, according to Manifest Destiny, the Americans were always destined to liberate. With a motivated population largely united under the same goal, it is no surprise that the American economy boomed in the first half of the 19th century. The American Industrial Revolution soon followed the European one, borrowing the best of its characteristics and fusing them with its newly acquired national identity.

Although America's economic growth was supported by a population boom and some prosperous decades, the creation and development of new industries and societies slowly started to split the country in half. This divide would prove to be fatal for America's future. The cracks started to form within the American public, and it was based not only on geography but also on societal and political differences.

Chapter 2 – The North and the South

In the previous chapter, we briefly touched on the North-South divide, which started to make itself apparent in the 19th century. The differences that emerged between the Northern and Southern states spread to almost all fields of life, and their severity increased to all-time highs. The American public became highly polarized and was divided on crucial social, political, and economic issues. In a way, the US abandoned the optimistic spirit that it had upheld since gaining independence.

This chapter will focus on the problems that caused a massive divide in the American public and depict the distinctions in the ordinary lives of Northern and Southern citizens of the country. These problems would cause the Civil War to break out in 1861.

The Mason-Dixon Line

Before we start examining the clear-cut distinctions between the North and the South, it is first vital to understand where the North and South actually began and ended. The border between the two sides was clear at the time of the Civil War, but the exact geography of the conflict cannot fully be considered as "Northern states versus Southern states." For example, California, although located in the west of the country, was considered a Northern state. The divide between the North and the South has implications that reach far beyond simple geography.

The Mason-Dixon Line was once a demarcation line that separated the American states of Pennsylvania, Maryland, Delaware, and Virginia. It gained a sort of symbolical significance decades after its creation in 1767 as a separation line between the Southern and Northern states. Roughly speaking, everything north of this line was considered a Northern state, sharing the same socio-political ideas. The states south of the Mason-Dixon Line were the Southern states, which often held opposing political ideas to the North.

The Mason-Dixon Line.
https://commons.wikimedia.org/wiki/File:Mason-dixon-line.gif

Along this line, the differences between the two sides started to show. Of the original Thirteen Colonies, seven of them—New Hampshire, Massachusetts, Rhode Island, New York, Connecticut, New Jersey, and Pennsylvania—were in the North, while the remaining six—Virginia, Delaware, Maryland, North and South Carolina, and Georgia—were in the South. However, this does not accurately reflect the positions of the states during the outbreak of the Civil War. For example, Delaware and Maryland sided with the North, despite being south of the original Mason-Dixon Line. Still, it is a nice starting point to have when drawing an imaginary line between the two sides.

The country's rapid industrialization and its expansionist efforts in the west slowly started driving a wedge between the Northern and Southern societies. The industrialization process was largely focused in the North instead of the South. States like Pennsylvania and New York were the forerunners in adopting and developing new industries. Their economic systems were almost entirely dependent on them. The vast river and canal systems of the North allowed for faster transportation of manufactured goods, which made the area naturally superior to the vaster and loosely connected South. Connecticut became a hub for America's manufacturing industries. It was located at the crossroads of all the Northern states and had access to the inland rivers and the ocean.

With the introduction of new machinery—one of the most important characteristics of the Industrial Revolution—many jobs that were previously done by hand were quickly being replaced, accelerating not only the production of refined goods from raw materials but also the general growth of different industries. The introduction of these new technologies transformed the American economy, just as had been the case in Europe decades earlier. Crucially, new farming devices, such as binders and reaping machines, were adopted to greatly increase efficiency, making up for the shortage of labor that plagued the country. In addition, the revolutionary invention of the cotton gin in the 1790s made the cotton-picking process easier, as it reduced the time needed to pick a pound of cotton from hours to minutes.

The South, on the other hand, had largely remained rural and based on agriculture. In fact, despite being rich in raw materials, Southern states had to send whatever they produced to the North for it to be refined and manufactured as goods. They would then buy the goods back for higher prices. The South was not really losing money during this process because of extremely high returns on agriculture and slave ownership, but its dependence on Northern industry was becoming more evident as the 19th century progressed.

As we have already mentioned, the very rich in the South had built such luxurious lives for themselves that the majority of the South was motivated to follow in their footsteps, thus causing a general slowdown in the urbanization process. The majority of the Southerners worked as farmers, and the products they grew they consumed or sold locally. Only the ones at the very top could export their materials in large quantities to other states. In the North, the citizens slowly started to move to the cities en masse and work for wages. Meanwhile, the Southerners were hesitant to give up their life's work and just abandon the holdings of which they had grown so proud.

This last factor proved to be a serious problem. Despite the fact that the Southerners aspired to become rich slave owners and enjoy lavish lives on their plantations, the majority of them never reached the same levels as the ones on the top. The wealth distribution in the South was extremely unequal, with only a minority being planters—slave owners with more than a hundred slaves. There were only about fifty thousand people in total out of an estimated five million people. Per capita, the Southern citizens were wealthier than their Northern counterparts. Despite not all of the Southerners enjoying similar privileges and riches as the slave owners, the majority who owned land made great yearly profits and had enough to live comfortably.

Land ownership was crucial for the Southerners, who grew different crops. Cotton—the crop most associated with slavery—was not the most common among slave owners, although it was arguably the most valuable material. Due to the particular conditions required to grow cotton in large numbers, it was only harvested in what's called the Lower South: Georgia, the Carolinas, and Texas, albeit to a smaller degree. Other Southern states grew tobacco, like Virginia. Along the Mississippi, the most common crop cultivated by slaves was sugar.

When comparing the more urban areas of the South with the North, the differences are just as evident. Despite the fact that Southern citizens were just as, if not comparatively, wealthier than their Northern counterparts, most of them lived in rural areas. The economy of the South was so reliant on the citizens' agrarian lifestyle that the urbanization process was greatly halted. Most of the Southerners refused to move their lives to newer towns and cities. Meanwhile, in the North, big cities like New York and Philadelphia were quickly growing, both in size and in population. For example, two of the largest cities of Virginia—Richmond and Petersburg—only had up to about sixty thousand people by the time the war broke out. Chicago, St. Louis, and Cincinnati, which were relatively newer cities, each contained a population of more than 100,000.

When it came to urban areas, most people in the South lived in New Orleans, a city that has nowadays become synonymous with African American culture. Back in the 18th century, it was one of the largest slave ports. The truth is that the South simply could not keep up with the North's growth. The North experienced rapid industrialization, but the South over-glorified and over-relied on the agrarian lifestyle. This had spill-over effects in areas of life, such as the general education level. By the 1860s, a fifth of the Southern citizens were illiterate, not taking into consideration the slaves who made up nearly half of the South's population. Comparatively, about 95 percent of Northerners had at least some type of education. As for the youth, only a third of the Southern children went to school in comparison to the three-quarters in New England and the Midwest.

The Slavery Question

The population boom of the early 19th century did not only include the white citizens of the United States, whose ranks were reinforced by the influx of immigrants who arrived in the country in search of new, prosperous lives. The slave population also increased dramatically in the first few decades of the 1800s but only in the South. While the North was becoming wearier of slavery as a practice and was abandoning the old agrarian lifestyle to pursue new opportunities in cities, the Southerners were happy to continue acquiring more land and expanding their properties. This meant that more slaves were needed to work those lands, and in many cases, they were transported from the Northern states that now had little use for them.

Over time, the planters with the most slaves competed with each other, comparing who provided the best and worse conditions for their slaves—something that is a complete exaggeration since the slaves lived under terrible circumstances no matter what their masters thought.

Christianity had an immense influence on the cultural lives of the slaves. The slaves didn't lose their culture; instead, it evolved, borrowing from the American lifestyle and from long-lasting African traditions to create a unique, rich culture. By the early 19th century, the slave population was predominantly Christian, a consequence of the God-fearing South.

However, as the oppressed blacks increasingly converted to Christianity, the churches found it difficult to accommodate them due to their status as slaves. In reality, the whole slavery ordeal was a pretty unchristian matter, and ignoring that fact was very difficult at times. Black Christianity became a cultural phenomenon, incorporating traditional African elements, such as passionate choir singing and dancing, into Christian rituals. In such a religiously diverse place like the United States, where Christianity had multiple variations and separate churches, not everyone welcomed blacks in their ranks. Some, like the Baptists, were more indifferent about blacks taking part in sermons or regular Christian activities. Black Christians even found themselves as preachers in the churches that welcomed them.

Finding joy and freedom in religion was crucial since it signaled that the oppressed black population had a place to experience true happiness despite living such miserable lives. Religion also somewhat boosted the literacy of the slave population. Although some slaves, mainly those who had day-to-day contact with their owners, were taught by their masters to read and write, most of the slaves who were literate came about as a result of Christians who genuinely wanted the oppressed to learn more about God's deeds.

Another side effect of a growing slave population that was becoming more literate was the creation of special groups of white men called patrols. Interestingly, as the decades passed, slave rights somewhat increased, despite the fact they were still being very much oppressed. For instance, slaves could practice their religion in certain white churches. Over time, slaves were sometimes permitted to leave their master's property. They typically had to have a written pass signed by their owner permitting them to leave for a given time. Patrols were hired by larger slave owners who wished to control the activities of their slaves when they went off their property. The patrols would check the passes of the roaming slaves to see whether or not they had been permitted to leave. If the slaves did not have a permit, the patrollers would violently beat them to teach a lesson. It was yet another measure to try and monitor the slave population as effectively as possible. Recent developments had aroused some suspicion in the slave owners, who feared a large enough slave rebellion might overthrow them from power.

Slave rebellions were nothing new at the time. The famous Haitian Revolution is perhaps the most obvious example in which a predominantly black population gained control through an armed revolt. South America had also seen a couple of instigations in Brazil and Guiana. In the US, the most alarming slave revolt took place in 1831 in Southampton County, Virginia. Led by an enslaved young man by the name of Nat Turner, the Southampton Insurrection was ultimately unsuccessful at undermining the slaves' oppression. It cost the lives of about two hundred blacks and one hundred whites. The rebellion was violently crushed and started a new wave of legislation that sought to further limit the rights of the slave population.

The rebellion of 1831 was perhaps the first time the Southern slave owners were terrified. Their society was dominated by blacks, the majority of which were young men who theoretically could seize control if they managed to achieve high levels of mobilization. To avoid the worst possible scenario from developing, the Southern slave owners spread pro-slavery propaganda. For example, they claimed that slavery was the natural condition of the blacks, something that had been decided by God when he was creating whites as the "natural superiors." Still, the Southampton Insurrection lit a spark in the United States, which quickly spread like wildfire in the following decades.

First Signs of Abolitionism

After the Southampton Insurrection, the anti-slavery movement took off around the nation, especially in the North. Although the movement did not see much success at first, during the 1830s, more people started vocalizing their opinions, believing that the government should eventually do something to prohibit slavery once and for all. Many stated that it was the "right thing to do" or that it had worked in the Old World. Before the insurrection, a common opinion was that slavery would eventually die off. For example, the new machines that had been invented during the Industrial Revolution would eventually replace the human labor that was performed by slaves.

There were no talks of completely freeing the enslaved black population, let alone giving them sufficient rights, but more people slowly recognized the terrible things slavery stood for and how it impacted the social and political development of the country. The most optimistic citizens trusted the US government to implement new policies that would be along the same lines as the abolition of the slave trade, which had been passed in 1808.

It has to be mentioned that, despite having abolished the importation of slaves to the country in 1808, Congress also made decisions that pleased the Southerners. For instance, in 1820, an act known as the Missouri Compromise permitted Missouri to enter the Union as a slave state. Maine would be admitted as a free state, and slavery would be banned from the rest of the lands acquired from the Louisiana Purchase that fell north of the 36° 30' parallel. Before its enactment, the issue of slavery had risen in importance. The legislation was a way of immediately dealing with the matter, but it was by no means a long-term solution to the problem.

The Missouri Compromise.

The Missouri Compromise established some rules regarding the future admission of US states, with both the free North and the slave-owning South agreeing that upsetting the balance between the free and slave states would be detrimental to the country. After 1820, the balance was supposed to be kept equal, and for a time, it was: there were twelve free states in the North and twelve slave states in the South. But the compromise affected the future expansion of the US. As states were added to the Union, the number of slave states would grow just as much as the number of free states. At the time, nobody cared enough to address the matter permanently, and the Missouri Compromise was the law of the land for over a decade.

However, in the 1830s, the socio-political climate had almost completely changed. The advocates for abolitionism became more organized and started publicly voicing their opinions. For example, in 1831, a journalist named William Lloyd Garrison founded a newspaper by the name of *The Liberator* in Boston. It was one of the first publications that were clearly anti-slavery, and it started a snowball effect in the North. Intellectuals, politicians, and regular citizens who believed in the cause concentrated on attacking the practice of slavery. In 1833, three years before two new states were inaugurated into the Union (Arkansas in the South and Michigan in the North), William Lloyd Garrison helped establish the American Anti-slavery Society in New York. It was a public space intended to discuss abolitionism as a whole and provide an avenue for abolitionists to voice their opinions. It promoted anti-slavery practices in the North and was pretty successful, quickly gaining followers in the big Northern states.

Slowly but surely, a sizeable anti-slavery movement gained traction in the nation, something that alarmed the Southerners who relied so much on the slaves they owned. What boosted public sentiment against slavery were the reports of fugitive slave cases. Slaves who escaped were called fugitives, and if they were caught, they would be returned to their owners. The First Fugitive Slave Act of 1793 permitted local governments to capture and return escaped slaves to their previous owners and punish those who were involved in their flight in any way. Reports of slaves, who had escaped years before, being captured, brutally treated, and then transported back to the plantations against their will continued to shock the abolitionist North and fueled the anti-slavery movement.

What is interesting is that by the time the Civil War broke out in 1861, the issue of slavery had, in a way, transformed into something more than just the North advocating for abolition and the South protecting the practice. As the two sides' opinions on the matter matured over the decades, a pattern started to develop, especially in the higher societies in the North. Most Northerners did not support giving blacks the same rights they held, as it was a way of still distinguishing themselves as superior. Thus, a sense of racism certainly characterized Northern society.

Despite this, the North was ashamed of the fact that the United States claimed to be a bulwark in the free, Western world but still practiced slavery to a large extent. They wanted to abolish the institution and change the Constitution but were not keen on pushing the anti-slavery movement further than that.

As for the South, we have already mentioned that the image that has become associated with a typical 19th-century American Southerner—a rich planter with a large mansion and acres of land worked by slaves—only represented a minority of all slave owners. One could argue that many Southerners were hopelessly trapped in a vicious cycle. They wished to live the same lavish lifestyles as the ones on the very top, but they were largely unsuccessful. However, once they got involved with the slave business, it was very hard to stop. Slavery was a demanding practice; it demanded constant time, energy, and resources to maintain and expand the "business." The slave owners' attention, no matter their social status or the number of slaves they owned, was almost totally focused on controlling their properties. Personally attending to the management of their slaves was a truly tiresome experience and a burden to many. The system that had been established in the United States by the 1860s required slave owners to be careful of every decision they made since it might affect the way their slave business would develop in the future.

When the Civil War broke out in 1861, it became clear that, despite all the negatives that came with being a slave owner, the Southerners were still ready to defend what they considered was their right.

Chapter 3 – Rising Tensions

The divide between the North and the South continued to expand, and it became clear by the 1850s that the two parts of the country were almost completely different in nearly all regards. The North was highly urbanized and educated, with more people choosing to work wage-paying jobs. The North was more modernized, not only economically and technologically but also socially. The Northerners developed new social groups and advocated for pursuing principles that had been described as the main pillars of the United States. The South, on the other hand, was hesitant to give up the agrarian lifestyle it had developed for decades. The Southerners continued to be reliant on land and slave ownership. The tensions between the two sides had long existed and showed themselves time and time again, sometimes by citizens but mostly in Congress, where representatives from Southern and Northern states clashed with each other on practically every issue.

With this background in mind, get ready to explore the decade leading up to the breakout of the Civil War.

A Brief Recap of the Mexican-American War

Before we discuss the laws that played a major role in shaping the United States in the 1850s, we must first take a look at an event that greatly influenced the country. The Mexican-American War was waged from April 1846 to February 1848. It was perhaps the single biggest occurrence that indirectly caused the Civil War. The Mexican-American War had both short- and long-term consequences that shook up the socio-political and economic lives of average Americans.

The war between Mexico and the United States ended in a US victory. It was fought over the issue of Texas, a Mexican region that became increasingly inhabited by American immigrants during the first part of the 19th century. The proximity of Texas to the South, coupled with the richness and vastness of its lands, meant that it was quite easy and, in some sense, even desirable for the average American to venture there and settle down. Mexico even encouraged immigration to some extent, although it might be better to say Mexico did not have enough time or energy to properly address the situation since it was caught up in constant conflicts throughout the first decades of the 1800s. Mexico first fought to gain independence from Spain, and then the Mexicans struggled throughout the 1820s and 1830s since the country could not settle on what kind of rule was best. Texas was one of the biggest provinces of the country back then by pure land size. It was so far away from the heart of Mexico that it was largely unpopulated, which was yet another factor that allowed the American settlers to move freely into the territory and start new lives.

The Americans were barely monitored by the Mexican government. Over time, any attempt to enforce some sort of regulating legislation was simply ignored by those who had immigrated. By the mid-1830s, it had become clear there was nothing left in Texas that could be considered purely Mexican. The Americans dominated the province and constituted the majority of the population. In addition, they were mostly Protestant. Mexico, on the other hand, was one of the most Catholic nations in the world by that time. Mainly, there was the ever-so-relevant question of slavery. Slavery was technically banned in Mexico, but the Americans who lived in Texas still practiced it without any real limitations.

Eventually, after a constant back and forth between the two sides, Texas rebelled against the Mexican regime in October 1835. The rebellion was ultimately successful. The Texans fought fiercely. They were led by Sam Houston and reinforced by some American volunteers who aided their co-nationals in their virtuous cause. Texas managed to gain independence, organizing the short-lived Republic of Texas in March 1836.

The formation of the Republic of Texas was devastating for Mexico. Mexico's internal struggles multiplied after the loss of such a large territory. The high command under General Santa Anna tried to hide the news of the defeat but was unsuccessful in doing so. The country did not have the resources to retaliate, and constant domestic troubles made it impossible for Mexico to focus on recapturing the lost territory. However, it never officially recognized Texan independence.

Regardless, the Texans rejoiced. They modeled their country, legislation, and general political system after the US. They even had their own congress and senate. As the days passed, it became clear that the majority of the population wanted to officially become part of the United States. It made sense. Most Texans were American-born, believed and lived by American principles, and lived right next to the American people. In addition, the United States had been seen as a natural ally to Texas, especially since many Americans had fought side-by-side with the people of Texas in its revolutionary war as volunteers. The US was also the first country to formally recognize Texan independence.

However, the situation was not that simple in the US, despite the fact that the majority of the public advocated for the annexation of the territory and its inauguration as a state. After all, it was the age of Manifest Destiny and American expansionism. But annexing Texas would mean that a new slave state would enter the Union, which would upset the balance that had been agreed upon in the Missouri Compromise in 1820. It would greatly displease the North, which no longer supported slavery. Although another northern state could have been theoretically formed from the Indiana Territory, Texas was far more organized and developed, giving a natural edge to the South.

Eventually, thanks to the efforts of newly elected President James K. Polk, Congress would be swayed to annex Texas as a new state in 1845. Polk was enthusiastic about US westward expansion and a firm advocate of Manifest Destiny. His whole presidential campaign had been based on the annexation of Texas. What served as the dealbreaker was the matter of Oregon, another US territory at the time whose ownership was being disputed with Great Britain, which bordered it to the north. Through negotiations, Polk was able to secure Oregon. It officially became a territory in 1848, but he convinced Congress to sign an annexation act in late 1844.

The Texans ratified the treaty with overwhelming public support in early 1845 and officially entered the Union in February of the next year. But naturally, this process did not go unnoticed by Mexico. The Mexican government, desperate for any sort of successful showing, vehemently opposed the annexation of Texas by the US. The country even made several threats to the US, signaling that it believed the annexation of the province to be unjust. There was also the issue of the border that separated Mexico from Texas, which had technically been agreed upon by the two sides after the revolution in 1836. However, it was not respected by either side. Texans claimed they controlled the territory up to the Rio Grande, despite the fact that the farthest Texan settlement was not far from the Nueces River, which Mexico claimed to have been the boundary.

The situation escalated when President Polk sent troops to the disputed area to reinforce the border, suspecting a potential Mexican attack. This was seen as a complete humiliation to the Mexican people, who thought that war was inevitable. In the end, a Mexican scouting vanguard attacked the US patrol on the disputed border in an encounter known as the Thornton Skirmish in April 1846. The two sides went to war.

It was clear from the very beginning that the United States would eventually triumph—and triumph it certainly did. By attacking multiple fronts and stretching the Mexican resources thin, the US forces attained a relatively easy and quick victory against the Mexicans, who neither had the heart nor the necessary resources to resist adequately.

While a portion of fighting was going on at the Texan border, the US fleet and Western Expeditionary Forces also swept into California and the Santa Fe Trail, undermining Mexican defenses and exposing the left flank. Under General Winfield Scott, the main US force landed in eastern Mexico and made its way to Mexico City, rolling over the Mexican troops in the process. The Mexicans finally surrendered about two years later. They signed the devastating Treaty of Guadalupe-Hidalgo, which ended the war and gave the US total control of the territories it had occupied in the conflict. The United States agreed to pay $15 million in physical damages—an amount that meant nothing compared to what the country had gained.

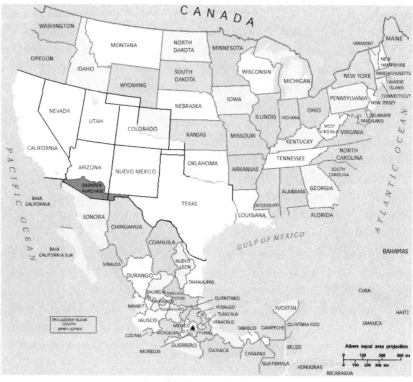

Mexican cession.
https://commons.wikimedia.org/wiki/File:Mexican_Cession_in_Mexican_View.PNG

Implications of the War

The Mexican-American War was, for the most part, an easy victory for the United States. According to the Treaty of Guadalupe-Hidalgo, the United States assumed possession of about one-third of all Mexican territories. Basically all of the modern Southwest was seized by the Union, including the states of New Mexico, California, Nevada, Utah, and Colorado. It was a massive victory for Manifest Destiny and US expansionism. The American "dream" of connecting the East Coast and the West Coast by land had come true.

However, the country found itself in a dilemma. These new territories meant they would eventually be inaugurated into the Union as states. It was a massive deal for both the North and the South since an expansion of this magnitude could give a significant advantage to one of them. The Southern slave owners wanted more slave states. They would have more room to expand in the west, which meant more opportunities for land, which, in turn, meant more income through agriculture and slave ownership. They knew that establishing slavery in unsettled lands meant they would be free to pursue their goals without much regulation. On the other hand, the North hoped to gain control of the western lands. Not only would it limit the potential expansion of slave states and further diminish the practice in the future, but it would also cut off the South from access to the Pacific. The industrialist North wanted to have reliable trade routes to new Asian markets.

In short, both sides eyed the territories for themselves. It was becoming clear that Congress could not stall much longer; they had to address the pressing issue. Even before the end of the war, Congress discussed the matter. In August 1846, about four months after the start of the war, many high-society members, those who were directly and indirectly involved with the war, had already recognized that it would only be a matter of time before the US emerged victorious. Congressmen in both the Whig and Democrat parties were thinking about what to do with the territories obtained in the war. They were also split within their parties themselves, with different representatives of both parties having different opinions.

On August 8th, 1846, President Polk submitted a bill to Congress requesting $2 million for negotiations with Mexico. Polk's administration thought that it was apparent, even in the first four months of the war, that the US would win, so they wished to please the anti-war opposition by quickly resolving the matter through negotiations. In hindsight, they greatly overestimated the matter, as the Mexicans, despite being at a significant disadvantage, lasted for another year and a half.

Still, before Congress voted on whether or not it would satisfy the president's request, a group of Democrats, led by David Wilmot of Pennsylvania, hurried to add a very important point. Wilmot, who was a sympathizer of Polk's administration, and a group of like-minded congressmen proposed to add an amendment that would prohibit the practice of slavery in all lands that would be acquired from Mexico. The Wilmot Proviso, as the amendment came to be known, was modeled after the Northwest Ordinance of 1787, when Congress adopted a similar law regarding the territories of what is now the Midwest (those that would later be organized into Ohio, Indiana, Illinois, Michigan, Wisconsin, and Minnesota). Wilmot and his supporters wanted the proposal to be added to President Polk's bill so the matter could be voted on.

At first, some Democrats proposed that instead of the no-slavery point applying to the territories, the Missouri Compromise line should simply extend along the 36°30' latitude all the way west to the Pacific, with all territories north of the line remaining slavery-free. However, this proposal was voted down by the House. The House passed the vote to add the Wilmot Proviso to the president's bill, which was successful. The passing of the bill could have major implications on the future of slavery in the US, so the Southern congressmen attempted to kill the bill by postponing or "tabling" it. They failed. The passing of the bill, including the proviso, was put up to vote in the House, and it passed, although just barely, with eighty-five votes for and eighty against. All that was left was for the Senate to ratify it.

However, despite being passed in the House, the Senate never passed the bill containing the Wilmot Proviso. In fact, they never passed any amendment that would prohibit the practice of slavery in the newly acquired territories from Mexico. Vehemently opposed by pro-slavery Whigs and Democrats, the senators for the proviso were always outnumbered, and the votes never fell along party lines. The bill reappeared at the end of the year during the president's renewed request for funds, but the proviso never saw success in both the House and the Senate. Some argued that deciding what to do with the territories prior to actually acquiring them was useless and created more confusion. Some returned to the proposal of simply extending the Missouri Compromise line, but the Southerners did not agree. They realized that about two-thirds of the country would fall north of the line and saw it as a defeat.

The United States entered the 1850s with a highly polarized political climate and a considerable chunk of new territories. The country could barely keep the balance of slave and free states, and now there was great uncertainty regarding the acquired lands. It seemed as if the future of the country would be decided upon in the coming years.

Addressing Post-war Issues

Although the Wilmot Proviso failed to pass, it provides an example of how anti-slavery sentiments had significantly grown in the past years, something that can partially be attributed to the establishment of new abolitionist groups, newspapers, and clubs in the North. The proviso also symbolized the tragic resistance to the matter of ending slavery in newly acquired territories. Still, the Northerners had significant grounds to believe their efforts of fighting against slavery could finally come true.

In 1848, Whig candidate Zachary Taylor narrowly squeezed out a victory in the presidential election. The problem with his candidacy was that the country had not figured out what to do with the territory acquired in the war, and Taylor didn't support a certain camp. His careful campaign pleased both the pro-slavery Southerners, with Taylor promising to take into consideration their economic interests of creating slave states out of the new territories, as well as abolitionist Northerners, who were swayed by Taylor's promises to leave the slavery question largely up to the populations of the newly acquired territories.

Several crucial developments in the late 1840s determined how the congressional debate over the new lands would go in the following years, such as the discovery of gold in California. Before Taylor took office in late 1848, gold was discovered in the region, quickly transforming California from a distant "promise land," where only the bravest dared to venture to start new lives, to the hottest commodity in the country. The discovery of gold started the famous California Gold Rush, which saw hundreds of thousands of people swarm to the west to gain access to the region's riches. This raised the importance of California to the top of the agenda, making it stand out among the other newly acquired lands from the Mexican-American War.

The problem, however, lay in the fact that since California still did not have an official territorial government, despite President

Polk's efforts in his last months in office, there were no real laws regulating the collection of its valuable resources. California, like most of the US Southwest acquired in the war, was still under the control of the military, which could only do so much in terms of official legislation. There was an urgent need to set up an official governmental body, either in the form of granting California the status of an organized US territory or skipping that stage and making it a state. The California Constitutional Convention of 1849 further demonstrated public support for this claim. More crucially, the people wanted to outlaw slavery in all of California, disregarding the Missouri Compromise, which would have split the state into two.

There was also the Texas question, or rather a question of its ever-so-problematic borders. Mexico had agreed to recognize the border along the Rio Grande, but that part was not the problem. Texas still claimed a large chunk of land in the north and northwest, which New Mexico disputed. This claim was largely baseless since Texan control never really spread to the lands it claimed. In addition, many New Mexicans were upset about being included with the Texans due to ideological differences. It was no surprise that the two sides were not on good terms with each other, with their differences going back to the Santa Fe Expedition of 1841 when a Texan force unsuccessfully journeyed northward to secure the disputed territories of the valuable Santa Fe Trail. Also, New Mexico, being largely populated by people of Hispanic origin, did not allow slavery, unlike Texas, which was one of the largest US slave states at that time.

Although the territorial issues of California and Texas were higher up on the agenda, they were not the only ones that required the government's immediate attention. The growth of the anti-slavery movement had caused a rising dissatisfaction toward the practice of slavery in the country's capital: Washington, DC. Located right on the historic Mason-Dixon Line, Washington held immense symbolic importance. For the North, the fact that the practice of slavery was permitted in the capital was humiliating for the country's international image. The South, on the other hand, saw great pride in it, believing Washington to be "on its side."

Concerning slavery, there was another matter that required settling. After the rising anti slavery sentiment, the number of slaves who escaped from their masters in search of freedom greatly increased. They would head north, hoping to reach the free states and start new lives. The North was becoming so unsympathetic toward slavery in general that, in many cases, even if escaped slaves were found in the North, people would not send them back to their previous owners, defying the Fugitive Slave Act. The Northerners passed personal liberty laws, which diminished the power of the Fugitive Slave Act of 1793. They had the legal right to act however they wished when coming across a fugitive slave. This upset the Southerners a great deal, and many representatives of the slave states pushed for new legislation to fix the matter. The prices of slaves were at an all-time high, and the North was constantly pressuring the practice however it could, so losing a single slave could make quite a dent in the pockets of the Southern planters.

The Compromise of 1850

As you can see, President Taylor and his administration had quite a lot on their plate, with different influential congressmen proposing different solutions to the problems. Out of these issues, the one that seemed the most inevitable was California's inauguration into the Union. The Californians had already expressed their desire to join the Union, so the Taylor administration had something to work with there.

But it would be three men—John C. Calhoun, Henry Clay, and Daniel Webster—who would lead one of the most influential debates on the issues in Congress. The trio, along with some other great politicians of early 19th-century America like John Quincy Adams, are considered to be the torch carriers of the Founding Fathers, a "Great Triumvirate" of politicians. They advocated for the development and promotion of the principles that shaped the lives of everyday Americans in that period.

Henry Clay.
https://commons.wikimedia.org/wiki/File:Henry_Clay.JPG

After rigorous negotiations behind the scenes, Congress had a general idea of what to expect. Henry Clay, a charismatic Whig from Kentucky who had matured in political debate during his time acting as secretary of state, presented eight bills on the floor of Congress in late January 1850. Clay had an infamous reputation among politicians of his caliber. He notoriously owned slaves and resided in a slave state; however, he believed that the future of the country lay in a slave-free society and was for gradual emancipation. He was quite different from many other representatives from Southern states but was still respected a great deal in both the North and the South. His past involvement in politics had earned him the nickname of the "Great Compromiser."

Thus, when he stood before the House to present his eight-part bill that addressed all the problems Clay saw relevant for the future of the country, he did what he did best—offered a compromise. Clay proposed admitting California to the Union as a free state, the establishment of the territories of New Mexico and Utah, debt relief for Texas in return for the state giving up its claims on the disputed borders, and, perhaps most importantly, suppression of the slave trade in the capital in return for a revisiting and implementation of stricter laws concerning fugitive slaves. Clay's bill hoped to please both sides, as usual, and it did to some extent. However, in the end, it fell through, opposed by some Northern Whigs and Southern Democrats.

The debate unfolded completely differently than how some might have imagined, and it lasted for seven months. At that time, both President Taylor and John C. Calhoun passed away, neither one seeing the final form of one of the most historic bills in US history. Taylor was replaced by Vice President Millard Fillmore, while Calhoun's emotional and influential speech shortly before his death was delivered to his colleagues by Senator James M. Mason. Calhoun was one of the firmest supporters of slavery and devoted much of his political career to defending and justifying it as a whole. It can be argued that his speech and the influence he had on his colleagues dragged out the debate for another couple of months.

President Fillmore sympathized with Clay's proposal: a new compromise to try and solve all the problems for both the North and the South while not taking a side. Clay had to leave Congress due to tuberculosis, and he was succeeded by Senator Stephen A. Douglas. Together, Fillmore and Douglas were able to convince the Texan representatives to give up some claims regarding the disputed borders with New Mexico, claiming that it was the responsibility of the United States to protect the rights of New Mexicans. In exchange for debt relief, Sam Houston of Texas and his supporters agreed to adjust the borders. The Senate passed the bill with support from both the Whigs and the Democrats; the only opposition came mainly from the South. Clay's proposal had finally seen the light.

The rest of the bills turned out to be far easier to gain support for. The organization of New Mexico and Utah as two new formal territories was not really opposed by either side, and the South agreed to the admission of California and the restriction of slavery in Washington in exchange for a stricter law on fugitive slaves. That was the whole point of the compromise in the first place. The Northerners got a new free state, limited the expansion of slavery to the Pacific Coast, and limited slavery-related activities in Washington. The Southerners got laws that made it easier for them to get hold of escaped slaves and settled the matter of Texas. In the end, both sides were not fully satisfied.

In September 1850, a historic package of five laws was passed as one bill. It became known as the Compromise of 1850, and it hoped to adequately address the two main concerns that had shaped the 19th-century United States: territorial expansion and slavery. Despite the fact that the "compromise" had been achieved, the extent to which it covered all the problems turned out not to be sufficient.

The admission of California as a free state was perhaps the clearest cut of the five points. There were no more questions left about the future state, and the matter was resolved pretty unanimously. However, the same cannot be said about other territorial issues. For instance, the bill and, to a larger extent, those who passed it had not yet decided what to do with the newly organized territories of Utah and New Mexico, mainly whether the two territories should be allowed to practice slavery. When the time came to split Utah and New Mexico into new states, it was known the debate on slavery would polarize the country even more. Still, this issue was largely ignored and postponed for future generations to decide.

The most attention was paid to redrawing the disputed borders between Texas and New Mexico—a matter that was arguably not nearly as important as the new restrictions regarding the slave trade in Washington, DC, or the expansion of the Fugitive Slave Act. According to new laws, buying and selling slaves were prohibited in Washington, DC, but owning slaves was still permitted. This did not make much sense, considering the inhabitants of the capital could simply take a short journey to the Southern states, buy their slaves, and then return home. The law was not beneficial to either side and was ultimately unsuccessful. The South was furious with the limitations put on Washington, while the North believed the only just way was the complete prohibition of slavery in every form.

As for the Fugitive Slave Act, the laws included in the Compromise of 1850 were blatantly pro-slavery. Upset and disappointed by the growing sentiment against the Fugitive Slave Act of 1783, the Southern slave owners demanded stricter control and monitoring of the fugitive slaves under the new legislation. They were perhaps more successful than what they might have hoped for initially. Under the new act, which went into effect in September 1850, fugitive slaves were prohibited from testifying on their own behalf—something that went against the democratic principles upon which the country had been based. Revoking the basic judiciary rights of escaped slaves was not as devastating as some of the other points. For instance, under new laws, people, regardless of their status or skin color, who were suspected of helping fugitive slaves escape from their owners were to be severely punished. Law enforcers all around the country, not only in the Southern states, were entitled to arrest fugitive slaves on just the basis of the claimant's sworn testimony, and they were required to assist the slave owners in finding their escaped slaves.

The new Fugitive Slave Act was undoubtedly the most shocking bill included in the Compromise of 1850, yet it got the least attention. It completely restricted whatever rights fugitive slaves had in the first place and was blatantly biased to please the planters of the slave states, who had grown distressed by the growing abolitionist movement. The act significantly swung the balance of power in their favor by changing the basic principles of the judiciary branch. For example, judges would be paid double if they found the fugitive slave guilty and returned them to their owners. It was totally undemocratic, but the legislators were so swept up in deciding the future of the newly acquired territories that they simply ignored what an immense implication this would have. However, the Compromise of 1850 achieved the opposite of what the Southerners had hoped. Instead of installing fear in the minds of the slaves, it exponentially increased the support of the abolitionist movement, prompting numerous Northern states to pass laws that would protect the individual liberties underlined in the act.

The Compromise of 1850 was perhaps the most important piece of legislation in antebellum America. Fresh out of a successful war against Mexico, Congress was once again unable to find a long-term solution to the most pressing issue in the country: the slavery divide. Instead, the compromise paid more attention to settling the individual squabbles between Texas and New Mexico and rushed the inauguration of California to the Union as a free state. On the other hand, the new Fugitive Slave Act and restrictions on the slave trade in Washington, DC, did not achieve their intended results.

They simply increased polarization on the subject. The two groups were becoming increasingly hostile toward each other, accusing the other of limiting their liberties and stagnating the country's development. For all these reasons, the Compromise of 1850 is often considered to be the beginning of the end for antebellum America.

The Kansas-Nebraska Act

The Compromise of 1850, despite its destructive consequences, was not regarded as destructive after its enactment. Instead of realizing that the public would be more divided on slavery after enforcing stricter laws on it, Congress believed that it had addressed the issue. This sentiment was shared and cemented by the next president, Franklin Pierce, whose 1853 inaugural address mentioned that the matter of slavery in the current and future territories of the United States was settled once and for all. Ironically, the following year would see Congress return to the issue of slavery once again. It was forced to implement new vital legislation in the unorganized territories of the country, something that was part of a larger deal, which was concerned with the further industrialization of the country through the construction of a crucial transcontinental railroad.

The debate on building a transcontinental railroad had been around since the early 1840s. All of Congress, both the Whigs and the Democrats, recognized the immense importance of this infrastructural project. The railroad was the future of transportation and the perfect way to travel long distances. There was no doubt that the country needed a railroad that would connect the east to the west, especially after the victory in the Mexican-American War brought new territories. However, as always, Congress could not come to terms with the exact details of the railroad's construction, such as where it would run and which states it would include. The North and the South both advocated for different routes, each excluding the involvement of the other states in the project. The only thing that was agreed upon was that the railroad should be financed by public land grants.

An important factor that played a big role in the debates over the construction of the railroad was the unorganized territory in the central part of the country, the territory that the United States had acquired through the Louisiana Purchase. In the 1850s, the leftover land that was still unorganized from the purchase was commonly referred to as "Nebraska." As new settlers found their way to the unexplored territory, there was a growing concern about implementing some kind of legislation. The matter of Nebraska should have been explored in congressional hearings, but nobody really had time for it. During most of the 1840s, the country's legislators were busy deciding what to do with the lands annexed from Mexico. Stephen A. Douglas, a Democratic senator from Illinois, had previously proposed organizing Nebraska into an official US territory and had tied in the construction of the railroad in his bill, but the bill never saw the light of day due to the issue of slavery. Most of the territory left over from the Louisiana Purchase fell north of the Missouri Compromise line, meaning that slavery would have been prohibited in those territories/states. The Southern legislators were no longer content with what had been agreed upon in 1820. In 1845, when Douglas first presented the bill, Southern politicians tabled it, urging Congress to divert its attention to more immediate issues.

After the Compromise of 1850, the issue of Nebraska became popular once again, with the House passing a bill in the spring of 1853 to organize it as a territory. The bill was then handed to the Senate. It seemed as if Douglas would finally be able to complete the organization of Nebraska. But it turned out that the Southern senators were not willing to let the matter just slide through. Realizing that the bill did not mention the future of slavery in the new territory west of Iowa and Missouri, they all united in voting against it. There was no mention of the allowance of slavery in Nebraska, which made it obvious that the authors of the bill had envisioned it to be a slave-free state since most of it lay north of the Missouri Compromise line. Led by Missouri Senator David Atchison, the Southerner senators united against the bill, and it was once again tabled. The Senate adjourned its activities, and both sides retreated to work on their strategies.

Once the Senate convened again in December, it was clear that Atchison and his supporters were not open to negotiating the terms of the deal. The South unanimously stood against the organization of Nebraska as a territory as proposed in the bill. This was mainly due to the fact that Nebraska and the railroad issue were increasingly connected with each other, and the Northerners would not let one pass without the other. Atchison and others were prepared to let the organization of Nebraska fall through, even if it was done at the cost of the transcontinental railroad.

The pressure was high on both sides. For the Southerners, the establishment of another territory (and eventually a state) north of the Missouri Compromise line would mean that their hopes of expanding slave territories were basically done for. On the other hand, the Northern senators, especially Douglas, placed more emphasis on the construction of the railroad, which would have given the North massive economic benefits since the railroad would start in Illinois. They also had a legislative edge over their opposition thanks to the Missouri Compromise.

In the end, what determined the fate of Nebraska, the transcontinental railroad, and the matter of slavery in the new territories was a point borrowed from the Compromise of 1850, which stated that the inhabitants of New Mexico and Utah would choose whether or not they would allow the practice of slavery by themselves. However, the two territories, although technically falling on both sides of the Missouri Compromise line, were never a part of the Louisiana Purchase, so whether or not slavery would be allowed there was not subject to the Missouri Compromise. Regardless, a new bill was proposed by Douglas in January 1854 that stated the same principle of popular sovereignty would apply to the Nebraska territory—those living in the vast area that spanned from modern-day Kansas to the US-Canadian border. But this created confusion in the Senate, with many believing that the deal would not be beneficial for the slave owners since it did not fully overturn the Missouri Compromise. Some Southerners thought that problems might arise in the future if they tried to expand their practices on such a vast chunk of land.

Kansas-Nebraska Act.
https://commons.wikimedia.org/wiki/File:McConnell%27s_historical_map_Kansas-Nebraska_Act,_1854.jpg

After another round of meetings between the two sides, which now also involved President Pierce, another version of the bill was proposed to the floor in late January. This time, it explicitly stated a complete repeal of the Missouri Compromise line and divided the original unorganized territory into two parts: Nebraska and Kansas. The justification of the first point was that the Compromise of 1850 had already, in a way, repealed the Missouri Compromise, so there was no need to keep enforcing it (although New Mexico and Utah had never been envisioned to be included by the legislation of 1820). The debate on the matter lasted for about four months and was not limited to Congress. Those in the North who believed in abolitionism took to the streets, organizing protests against the bill. The opposition to the bill, known as the Anti-Nebraska movement, believed that it was clearly pro-slavery and unconstitutional.

Despite harsh opposition, the Senate passed the bill with thirty-seven votes for and fourteen against, with fourteen senators from the free states voting in favor of it. It became clear once the House started its debate on the bill that it had become a sectional issue and that congressmen were no longer acting along party lines. All forty-five Northern Whigs opposed the bill, while the votes among the Northern Democrats were split forty-five in favor and forty-two against. The South was more one-sided, with sixty-nine votes for and nine votes against. On May 30th, 1854, President Pierce signed the Kansas-Nebraska Act into law.

Bleeding Kansas

The signing of the Kansas-Nebraska Act started a chain of events that led to more destabilization in the newly established territories, something that was further amplified by the divides between the Whigs and the Democrats. The act was a clear victory for the Southern slave owners. They believed they had a chance to do, thanks to the popular sovereignty clause that stated the inhabitants of the new territories were entitled to choose their slavery status. As immigrants from both camps started to flood Kansas and Nebraska, it became clear that instead of dealing with the pressing issue of slavery, Congress had once again avoided it, allowing the local population to decide for themselves. Although popular sovereignty sounded just at the moment (after all, the people who lived in the territory would be affected by the decision the most), the events that unfolded proved just how polarized the two sides were and to what extent they were ready to push their beliefs.

However, there never really was a "fair fight" on the rights of slavery when it came to Kansas. The majority of the new inhabitants were pro-slavery, organizing the town of Atchison in honor of the senator who had fought for the expansion of slavery during the debates on the act. Soon, Southern slave owners started to pour into Kansas en masse, trying to sway the upcoming vote in their favor and cement the territory's right to slavery. In a way, it was an organized effort by the Southern slave owners, who migrated from the nearby slave state of Missouri to fight for slavery. These men, who were often armed, were referred to as Border Ruffians. Their only motivation was to help Kansas become pro-slavery. Border Ruffians often raided and intimidated the population, forcing them to pledge allegiance to their cause and to vote against the prohibition of slavery in Kansas. It was a well-organized movement, but whether or not it had any real ties to the pro-slavery governments of the South is not known.

On the other hand, the abolitionists who settled in Kansas were just as resilient and focused. There were far fewer Northern immigrants, but they had settled in Kansas for the cause of abolitionism. The first abolitionist immigrants were praised by Northern media and politicians for their efforts, as they made the Kansas issue a matter of national significance. The abolitionists, often called Free Soilers, founded the towns of Topeka and Lawrence and posed a somewhat firm resistance to the Border Ruffians, despite being outnumbered.

The tensions between the two sides in Kansas escalated during the first election of its territorial legislature in March 1855. This election would be crucial in determining whether or not slavery would be allowed. The election, which took place on March 30th, was heavily influenced by the Border Ruffians, who arrived in large numbers from Missouri to take part in the vote and swing it in favor of pro-slavery candidates. Only two out of thirty-nine seats were won by abolitionist candidates. The Free Soilers protested the results and managed to convince the territorial governor to hold another election in May. They did see improvements but still lost the overall election, with nineteen seats going to the pro-slavery candidates.

In July, the pro-slavery legislature met in the town of Pawnee and drew up legislation, which was largely modeled on the bordering state of Missouri and allowed for the practice of slavery. On the other hand, the Free Soilers, who believed that the election was still fraudulent, convened in Topeka, creating their own version of the legislation and claiming it to be legitimate. By the end of the summer of 1855, there were two highly polarized camps in the Kansas Territory. Both sides handed their legislature to Congress to review and accept, but due to the support of pro-slavery President Pierce, the Free Soilers had no chance. The debate on the matter was postponed, and Congress appointed a special three-man committee to arrive in Kansas and assess the situation. A year later, after conducting a series of investigations and reviewing documents, the committee came to the conclusion that the original election of 1855 had been heavily influenced by non-resident Southern immigrants, who had only crossed the border into Kansas to vote for pro-slavery candidates. The committee declared that the pro-slavery legislation that had been drawn up was fraudulent and did not reflect the opinion of the majority of the Kansas residents.

However, the committee's decision did not change the highly polarized situation in Kansas. The two camps were still going strong, each believing to have been legitimate and now creating their own versions of a constitution to submit to the Senate. The divide soon transformed into an all-out armed confrontation between the Free Soilers and the pro-slavery Southerners.

After a Free Soiler was murdered by a pro-slavery Kansas resident in November 1855 (in a personal matter not related to politics), a series of armed confrontations erupted between the two sides. The pro-slavery Kansas militia, armed with stolen guns and a cannon, encamped near the Free Soiler town of Lawrence. Luckily, the governor of Lawrence managed to negotiate with the militia and avoided further escalation of the conflict.

At the same time, the Senate was busy reviewing the different constitutions of Kansas that had been submitted. The Topeka Constitution, drawn up by the abolitionists of Topeka, was rejected in early 1856, thanks to President Pierce, who said the Free Soiler government of Kansas was illegitimate (something that was partially disproved by the committee's findings). The Lecompton Constitution, which was pro-slavery, was next up, but the Free Soilers refused to show up to vote. The document was still presented to Congress for approval, but Congress sent it back, noting that it did not reflect the opinion of the majority of Kansas voters.

The third document to be reviewed by Congress was the Leavenworth Constitution, drawn up and passed by the Free Soilers. However, the Senate quickly killed the document since it was not only radically anti-slavery but also demanded voting rights for all male citizens, including blacks. The Wyandotte Constitution, another Free Soiler document, was drafted and sent to Congress for review in 1859. A popular representative referendum in Kansas miraculously approved the passing of the document in October 1859, but the Senate, still dominated by pro-slavery senators, tabled the bill.

As the debates in the Senate continued, so did the efforts of pro-slavery parties to eliminate and undermine abolitionist resistance in Kansas. In the infamous Sack of Lawrence, which took place in May 1856, hundreds of armed pro-slavery inhabitants from

Missouri openly invaded Kansas and sacked the abolitionist city of Lawrence. It was a brutal act of aggression—perhaps the first known armed conflict between the pro- and anti-slavery forces in the country. The situation did not die down. In the Senate, the abolitionists brought up the matter more and more. The debates became so heated that South Carolina Congressman Preston Brooks attacked Senator Charles Sumner from Massachusetts, nearly beating him to death. Although his actions were quickly condemned, it became clear that the issue of slavery in Kansas had penetrated into the mainstream and widened the divide between the North and the South.

The struggle for dominance between the Free Soilers and pro-slavery forces in Kansas continued until 1861, which was when Kansas was finally admitted to the Union as a free state. This followed the election of Abraham Lincoln as president and the secession of the Southern states from the Union. The six-year period of instability and high levels of polarization in Kansas is often referred to as "Bleeding Kansas." The events of Bleeding Kansas perhaps best describe the political situation in the country in the 1850s, a decade when pivotal decisions, such as the signing of the Compromise of 1850 and the Kansas-Nebraska Act, led to the start of the war between the North and the South.

Chapter 4 – The Republican Party

The signing of the Kansas-Nebraska Act was the final nail in the coffin for the sectional divides within the Democrats and the Whigs. Eventually, this divide caused the creation of the Republican Party, which managed to gain a lot of traction and has become one of the two most dominant political actors in the US today.

The Founding of the Party

In hindsight, when looking at the political climate of the United States after the Mexican-American War, it is clear that both the Whigs and the Democrats had significant problems within their parties. Due to the extreme divide over slavery, the views of the Whigs and Democrats were often not based on their party alignment but rather on where they were from. During the congressional debates, Northern and Southern Democrats and Whigs would often take similar stances on different issues rather than organizing their opinions based on their party's platform. It was very confusing and, to some extent, even unfair to the average voter.

The Whigs were so polarized that they could not reach any type of consensus when it came to slavery. The Southern wing of the Whigs was very conservative and had pro-slavery views, while the members of the newer anti-slavery wing increased in numbers throughout the 1850s. This divide had shown itself during the 1852 presidential election when the Whig candidate, Winfield Scott, a former general during the Mexican-American War, was crushed by Franklin Pierce, the Democratic nominee. A large portion of the Whigs had opposed Scott's nomination in the first place, something that became a pivotal factor in his ineffective campaign and eventual defeat.

After the passing of the Kansas-Nebraska Act, the divides within the Whig Party became more relevant than ever. Viewing the new bill as overwhelmingly pro-slavery, several anti-slavery Whigs, referred to as Conscience Whigs, decided to abandon their party and pursue their efforts independently. A new party was about to be founded in the United States that would quickly transform the political landscape of the country forever. A businessman and leader of the radical abolitionist wing of the party, Zachariah Chandler, and Salmon P. Chase and former President Martin Van Buren, leaders of the Free Soil Party, led the charge.

These like-minded individuals bonded together in the Anti-Nebraska movement, criticizing the passage of the pro-slavery act and urging others to join their cause. At the Anti-Nebraska meetings in Ripon, Wisconsin, in May 1854 and then in Jackson, Michigan, in July, they proposed officially forming a new party, one that would strive to oppose slavery in the territories. They called themselves the Republicans, borrowing perhaps from Thomas Jefferson when he first established the Democratic-Republican Party in 1792; it eventually dropped the second part of its name.

Free Soil, Free Labor, Free Men

The principles on which the newly created Republican Party stood for were a conglomeration of different ideas and values. Obviously, the opposition to the expansion of slavery was the central idea, one that attracted all of the members. However, it was not the only one. The Republicans envisioned a completely free United States, where slavery would be abolished in all the states, despite their history or economic reliance on the practice. To replace such a vast part of the country's economy, the Republicans advocated for the modernization of the US by, for example, building more factories and railroads and implementing a new banking system that would provide new opportunities for average citizens by giving them more flexible terms on loans. In addition, the Republicans also wanted to expand the country's agricultural sphere by gifting the undeveloped western lands to the farmers instead of selling them to already rich slave owners. The Republicans claimed well-functioning, capitalist free-market labor was the foundation and future of the United States. They pledged to do everything in their power to swing the country back to this long-abandoned course. The idea of "Free Soil, Free Labor, Free Men" was born and gave the Republican Party a unique set of values that differentiated it from the Whigs and the Democrats, who were still largely split on major issues.

Amidst the Bleeding Kansas events, the Republican Party organized its first national convention in Pittsburgh, Pennsylvania, in February 1856. There, the members of the party once again revisited and clearly defined their goals, which centered around the cause of fighting against the future expansion of slavery. It also clearly demonstrated their position of defending the Free Soilers of Kansas, who were under direct physical threat by their Southern opposition. The party also criticized President Pierce's overwhelmingly pro-slavery administration, condemning its reckless and hateful activities in the country.

In June of the same year, the Republican Party nominated its first presidential candidate: John C. Frémont. The former major of the US Army during the Mexican-American War, Frémont had played a big role in the Californian campaign and had made quite a name for himself after the end of the war by becoming rich from the California Gold Rush. Although Frémont did not manage to win the presidential election of 1856, he carried eleven states in total, all of which were in the North. He fell short to Democrat James Buchanan, whose campaign was ambiguous on the matter of slavery. The Whig candidate, Millard Fillmore, suffered a crushing defeat, only carrying one state and falling victim to the political chaos that had been established among the Whigs after the party's break-up.

Despite the defeat of the Republicans in the 1856 election, the party's future seemed promising. After all, in their very first election, they gained about a third of the popular vote. The party's success was largely attributed to its clear stance. Many people were drawn to the ideals of "Free Soil, Free Labor, Free Men" and knew exactly what they were choosing when they circled the Republicans on the ballot. Over the next few years, more politicians decided to join the Republican Party from both the Whigs and the Democrats, further contributing to its rise before the pivotal 1860 election.

Chapter 5 – The 1860 Presidential Election

The year 1856 was the last time a Whig candidate ran for election in a presidential race. Following the disintegration of the party, the Republicans became the second-largest political entity in the country. The next four years, up until the 1860 presidential election, were characterized by even more polarization between the pro- and anti-slavery camps. The 1860 presidential election had huge implications that forever changed the course of the country and directly led to the outbreak of the Civil War.

This chapter will briefly cover the most important events in the four-year period preceding the 1860 election, explore the election itself, and talk about some of the most immediate consequences of the election.

Dred Scott Decision

Democrat James Buchanan won the presidential election in 1856 with just over 45 percent of the popular vote. However, things were not looking good for his party or the Whigs. The latter had suffered a substantial split, with a number of its most influential members leaving the party to join the growing ranks of the Republicans. The Democrats still had no distinctive course to offer its voters. The issue of slavery was more relevant than ever, as the Bleeding Kansas events were happening concurrent to the election. But unlike former President Pierce, who had at least shown his support for the expansion of slavery in the Kansas Territory, Buchanan's administration was rather silent on the matter.

The slavery issue was further amplified by the famous Dred Scott case, which gained a lot of national attention in the 1850s. The final verdict was ruled just two days after Buchanan's inauguration. In short, Dred Scott was an African American man born in slavery in Virginia. He lived with his owner first in Alabama and later in Missouri. Eventually, Dr. John Emerson, an army surgeon, purchased Dred Scott from slavery in 1832 and took him first to Illinois—a free state—and then to Wisconsin—a slave-free territory according to the Missouri Compromise. Emerson traveled a lot but eventually returned to Missouri.

After the death of Emerson, Scott and his wife, Harriet Robinson, who was also a slave, tried to buy their freedom from Emerson's wife, Irene Sandford, who became their owner after the death of her husband. Irene rejected their bids, forcing them to file two separate lawsuits against her in April 1846 in Missouri, where they resided. The Missouri statutes at the time allowed African Americans to sue for wrongful enslavement. After a slave's arrival in a free territory, they automatically became free and should not be re-enslaved after reentering territories where slavery was legal. Missouri's famous motto was "once free, always free," and Scott and his wife hoped it would help them gain their freedom.

A photograph of Dred Scott.
https://commons.wikimedia.org/wiki/File:Dred_Scott_photograph_(circa_1857).jpg

However, in June 1847, the court ruled against them. In a retrial three years later, they managed to win their freedom. Irene Sandford was devastated by her loss and decided to appeal the case to the Missouri Supreme Court, combining the two separate lawsuits of Dred Scott and Harriet Robinson into one. She convinced the court to overturn the previous decision and reclaimed the ownership of Scott and Harriet in 1852. It was a spectacle and was swiftly followed by an appeal from Scott to the US Circuit Court in Missouri in December 1854, which he lost.

By that time, the case had gained the attention of many abolitionists, who helped Scott financially and provided legal services to him. With their support, Scott once again appealed the case, this time in the United States Supreme Court, the highest judiciary system in the country.

Despite fully believing that he was not in the wrong and despite all of the support from different abolitionist politicians and civil society figures, the Supreme Court denied Scott the right to his freedom on March 6ᵗʰ, 1857. The decision shocked the country and drove yet another wedge between the Northern abolitionists and the slave-owning Southerners. The case gained popularity due to the Supreme Court's justification. Led by Chief Justice Roger Taney, a Southerner, the Supreme Court made its decision based on two very debatable points. First, all people of African descent, regardless of whether or not they were a slave, were not citizens of the United States and thus were not entitled to sue anyone in federal court. Second, the Supreme Court found the Missouri Compromise of 1820, a piece of legislation that had determined the future of American expansion for over fifty years, unconstitutional. The Supreme Court not only rejected Scott's arguments but also basically said that Congress had no constitutional right to determine the expansion of slavery in the new territories.

The Dred Scott decision was a fatal ruling for antebellum America. It not only overturned a five-decade-long historic act, but it also managed to anger a significant portion of Americans. Northern abolitionists, white and black alike, protested the Supreme Court's decision, calling it unjust. They claimed (and not wrongfully) that the Supreme Court's final decision was not American in any sense and did not take into consideration the democratic principles on which the country was founded.

Thus, just two days after entering office, President Buchanan found himself and the whole country in a blazing fire that had been caused by the issue of slavery. The fate of Kansas was on the docket, and the Dred Scott decision greatly upset the abolitionists; it seems that Buchanan's term was doomed from the beginning. The North and South hated each other. It was a full-blown political crisis, with neither party willing to give an inch. It is not surprising that in the years following his inauguration, Buchanan and his administration were unable to introduce any effective measures to address the situation.

The Feud in the Democrats

The creation of the Republican Party was not only destructive for the Whigs. It was almost equally as bad for the Democrats, who had long been struggling among themselves and were perhaps the most polarized out of the two big parties in the country. The sectional divides in the Democrats were largely caused by the extreme pro-slavery wing of the party called the Fire-Eaters. Not only were these Southern Democrats the biggest advocates of slavery and its expansion in the US territories, but they also advocated for the secession of the Southern states from the Union. They believed that the differences between the North and the South had become unfixable and that the damage had already been done. The Fire-Eaters constituted only a minority of the party at the start of the 1850s but slowly grew in numbers as the Democrats gained more seats in the Southern states.

After eight years of mostly pro-slavery Democratic presidents, a number of Northern abolitionist Democrats had left the party by 1860 to join the Republicans. Still, some of the most prominent Democrats at the time, such as Stephen A. Douglas, remained and led the party through a tough four-year period after the election of James Buchanan.

In April 1860, the Democratic National Convention convened in Charleston, South Carolina. The main idea of the convention was to nominate the next presidential candidate to run for the party in autumn. By that time, the number of extreme pro-slavery members outnumbered the moderate and abolitionist members of the party. And since the convention was being held in Charleston, which was a Southern city, it was mainly attended by pro-slavery party members. Still, Douglas was the front-runner for the Democrat nomination, despite the fact that he was considered to be a member of the more moderate wing. He was perhaps the most distinguished member of the party, having worked extensively on the passing of the Kansas-Nebraska Act.

However, the Fire-Eaters vehemently opposed his nomination. They had prepared an extremely pro-slavery platform to be endorsed during the election. Among other points, it included clear support of the Dred Scott decision, a point that was instantly opposed by the Northern abolitionist Democrats. The abolitionists claimed that if such a platform was adopted, they would lose support in pivotal states, such as New York or Pennsylvania, making it almost impossible to win the election. Instead, a more moderate platform was adopted by a vote of 164 to 138, and it did not include the extremely pro-slavery parts. The Fire-Eaters protested. Led by

William Lowndes Yancey from Alabama, they walked out of the convention.

In total, fifty delegates from the Southern states left the Charleston convention, leaving those who remained unable to reach a consensus regarding the nomination of the next candidate since a two-thirds majority was needed. Douglas received 145.5 of the 253 votes cast and led the six other candidates for nomination; however, he still needed 56.5 more votes to be officially elected as the party's presidential candidate. In the end, the convention did not reach a consensus and adjourned to meet in six weeks in Baltimore to discuss the matter again.

The Democrats convened in Baltimore, Maryland, on June 18th, 1860, to nominate their candidate. However, 110 Southern delegates still boycotted the assembly, led by the Fire-Eaters, who did not attend it at all. The rest just walked out of the convention once they learned that the pro-slavery points would still not be included in the party's platform. The remaining Democrats were forced to resume the convention in the absence of the Southern delegates. Douglas managed to get the required two-thirds. However, the remaining delegates realized the severity of the situation and the fact that it would be near impossible to work with the Southern delegates. Still, they nominated Douglas as the Democratic presidential candidate for the 1860 election.

By that point, the extreme pro-slavery wing of the party had set up their own convention in Richmond, Virginia, on June 11th. When the Northern Democrats met in Baltimore, some Southerners decided to join them, but they left the assembly disappointed and returned back to Richmond, where they planned to nominate their own presidential candidate. Unsurprisingly, the first thing the Southern wing did was adopt the pro-slavery platform that had been rejected by the rest of the party. After unanimous approval of the platform, they nominated Vice President John C. Breckinridge as their candidate to run for president.

Although the whole situation was rather unusual and everybody recognized the problems associated with it, President Buchanan's administration was forced to accept two Democratic nominees. Buchanan had to endorse Breckinridge since he was the vice president; if he didn't, it would have been catastrophic for his administration's image. The president hoped that because of his endorsement, Breckinridge would win the electoral votes of his home state, Pennsylvania, which was a pivotal state in achieving victory in the election.

The sectional divides in the Democratic Party proved to be fatal for the party's future. Despite dominating the political landscape for the better part of the last twenty years, the Democrats were not able to deal with the problems between the Northern and Southern members of the party. Everyone knew that this split and the nomination of two candidates would be very difficult to overcome. Both camps were banking on getting electoral support in the North and South but failed to realize that their chances of winning the election were slimmer than ever. The newly formed Republican Party had gained the voters' attention by early 1860.

Republicans Nominate Lincoln

Things were looking up for the Republicans, whose numbers had only grown since the 1856 election. Unlike the Democrats, the Republicans were not sectionalized on the matter of slavery—well, at least not in the way the Democrats had been for decades. All Republicans opposed the expansion of slavery in the new territories acquired by the United States. However, some called for its complete abolition. This opinion separated the more moderate Republicans from the radicals, although the divide was not as extreme as the pro- and anti-slavery divide in other parties. In general, the Republicans opposed the practice of slavery, believing it to be harmful in the long term for the country's development. The main thing the party had to decide was which candidate would represent their views in the presidential race.

The Republicans held their convention in Chicago right after the failure of the Democratic convention in Charleston in May of 1860. In total, there were eight candidates that were running for the nomination. Out of them, four had perhaps the best chances: William H. Seward, the governor of New York who was considered to have been the main favorite; Salmon P. Chase, the governor of Ohio who had long opposed slavery; former Representative of Missouri Edward Bates, a conservative on the slavery issue and a slave owner himself; and, finally, Abraham Lincoln, the former representative of Illinois who had made quite a name for himself during the Lincoln-Douglas debates in 1858 but was not considered to have much of a chance against the likes of Seward.

The convention started out differently from what some had predicted. From the very beginning, it became clear that the big three—Seward, Chase, and Bates—had almost split the party since all three proposed very different party platforms that opposed each other. Due to his enthusiastic speech that supported the concept of nativism, Seward was seen as a radical on the anti-slavery matter. Although he did not mention the total abolition of slavery, Seward was perhaps misunderstood by his colleagues, causing him to lose a lot of supporters. Chase, on the other hand, voiced his unyielding anti-slavery views, which attracted a lot of radical abolitionists in the party. However, he did not have as much past experience and prestige as Seward, making his marketing as a potential candidate difficult. In addition, he did not have much support from the former Whig delegates of the party since he had been a former Democrat. Finally, Bates did not get much love from the majority of the party because he supported the expansion of slavery in the new territories, something that was considered unacceptable by most delegates.

This situation was well utilized by Abraham Lincoln, who, despite not being a clear favorite to win the nomination, had made quite a name for himself. Lincoln had long stated his anti-slavery views. In 1858, he spoke out on the matter on several occasions, including during the Kansas-Nebraska crisis in 1854 and after the Dred Scott decision. He had also gained quite a lot of popularity in Illinois, the state where he resided and pursued his political career in the House of Representatives.

Although Lincoln had always been actively involved in the political processes of his state, the biggest breakthrough of his career was perhaps the famous Lincoln-Douglas debates in 1858 when Lincoln and Stephen A. Douglas, who were both up for election as the representative of Illinois, toured the state and engaged in a series of seven debates on the matter of slavery. Lincoln, who was still relatively unknown outside of his state and firmly opposed the expansion of slavery in the new territories, challenged a veteran politician, Douglas, who advocated for popular sovereignty. Thanks to Lincoln's innate talent and charisma during his speeches, as well as his memorable posture and height of 6'4", Lincoln was able to effectively mesmerize his audiences and, in many instances, was named the informal victor of the debates. Although he ultimately lost the race, it was a close battle. The events of 1858 made him a favorite of the Illinoisans, who would assemble in the thousands to watch him give speeches.

Abraham Lincoln
https://commons.wikimedia.org/wiki/File:Abraham_Lincoln_O-77_matte_collodion_print.jpg

Having delivered an amazing speech three months before in New York, in which he carefully described the Republicans as the party where true American virtues were valued, Lincoln's views were well known inside of his party. The Cooper Union speech had been a massive success for Lincoln, who had not intended to use the platform to promote himself as a potential candidate. Instead, he wanted to give a thorough, honest run-down of his thoughts on crucial issues he believed needed to be addressed. The fact that the Republican convention was held in his home state was even more beneficial for Lincoln, let alone the fact that his three main opponents had not gained a significant edge over him for the spot of a nominee.

Although Lincoln did not attend the convention in person, he gained second place on the first ballot. Seward led the ballot, as predicted, but he could not manage to get the majority of the votes.

In the second round, Lincoln saw a significant increase in his votes, going from 102 to 181 delegates, although he still trailed Seward by three votes. By the third ballot, it was clear that Lincoln had gained the most support in the party, as he led Seward by more than fifty votes. Since a two-thirds majority was required to get the final nomination, a fourth ballot was held, and Lincoln was able to defeat Seward, gaining 349 votes in total and becoming the Republican presidential nominee for the 1860 election. Maine Senator Hannibal Hamlin was selected to run alongside him as vice president.

Election Results

In addition to Stephen A. Douglas and John C. Breckinridge from the Northern and Southern Democrats, respectively, and Abraham Lincoln from the Republicans, there was one other candidate who ran and managed to gain electoral votes. Former Tennessee Senator John Bell represented the Constitutional Union Party, which had been created by conservative Whigs after the collapse of their party. The former "Know-Nothings," members of the infamously xenophobic and nativist (Native) American Party that had operated in the country since 1848, were also involved in the Constitutional Union Party. ("Native" was dropped from the party's title in 1855.) After the creation of the Republican Party and the subsequent collapse of the Whigs, many of the former Whigs became members of the American Party, which stood against the immigration of Roman Catholic Europeans. The party believed they posed a threat to the economic and social prosperity of the Protestant United States. The Know-Nothings initially met in secret in New York City, and when asked about their secretive organization, they would often answer that they knew nothing, hence the name.

By 1860, the American Party had largely lost traction, and its members instead joined the upcoming Constitutional Union Party, which stressed the need to follow the US Constitution and follow the country's legislation. Due to the party's relative silence on the slavery issue and its members' conservative-leaning opinions, the Constitutional Union Party was particularly popular in the slave-owning South.

These four candidates clashed in the 1860 election. The Republicans and the Northern Democrats held a more anti-slavery stance, while the Southern Democrats and the Constitutional Unionists were more pro-slavery. Thus, in a way, there were two separate elections. The free North had to choose between anti-slavery Lincoln or Douglas since choosing openly pro-slavery candidates would be out of the question. The opposite went for the Southern voters, who had to make a selection between either Breckinridge or Bell, as voting for a clearly anti-slavery candidate would potentially impose direct changes to their lifestyles.

Due to these highly unusual circumstances, it should come as no surprise that there were some irregularities in the voting procedure. For example, Lincoln was not even on the ballot in ten of the Southern states and did not receive a single vote in 121 counties out of 145. Still, after the election ended on November 6th, 1860, Lincoln emerged victorious, thanks to the electoral college system of the United States.

Amassing just short of 40 percent of the country's popular vote, Lincoln got 180 electoral votes, all of them coming from states north of the Mason-Dixon Line, the Midwest, California, and Oregon. Comparatively, Douglas managed to gain the second-highest number of popular votes, coming in at about 29.5 percent, but he only carried two states—Missouri and New Jersey—which accounted for just twelve electoral votes. Breckinridge came third in the popular vote with just over 18 percent but second in the electoral vote, managing to gain seventy-two and winning in eleven states. Finally, Bell pulled a real rabbit out of his hat by gaining the least popular votes but still getting more electoral votes than Douglas and carrying three states.

The 1860 election still has one of the highest voter turnouts in the history of the United States, coming in at just over 81 percent. There were six states with a margin of victory under 5 percent and four with under 1 percent, making it one of the closest elections in the country's history. All four candidates had a genuine chance to win the election due to the electoral college, so it is not surprising that the final results further aggravated the political climate of the country. Abraham Lincoln, who did not even have 40 percent of all votes, was elected president of the United States.

Chapter 6 – Outbreak of the War

In 1860, the American people elected Abraham Lincoln as the president of the United States. Lincoln knew he would have to serve in an already hostile and extremely complex environment and realized he had to carefully plan every move that he wanted to make. Unsurprisingly, the first weeks after the election saw the country become more destabilized and divided, leading to the outbreak of an armed conflict between the Northern and Southern states.

The South Secedes

Although Abraham Lincoln earned the title of the "Great Emancipator" when he signed the Emancipation Proclamation on January 1ˢᵗ, 1863, he did not initially support the full abolition of slavery. Lincoln recognized just how much the Southern states were dependent on slavery. It was the heart of the South's economic and social life, and even though Lincoln had a clear anti-slavery stance, he knew the damage abolition would bring to the Southerners would be very difficult to overcome. What he and most of the Republican Party stood for, at least in 1860, was that slavery was an inherently plagued practice and that its expansion into new territories of the United States would be detrimental to the country's future in the long term.

Lincoln and others proposed a slow, gradual development of the country's economy so it would not be as reliant on slave labor. However, since the South was so used to slavery, it was very difficult to get this message across to the slave owners who had built up their fortunes thanks to slave labor.

So, when Lincoln became president, he faced immense opposition in the South. Not a month had passed after his election that the thoughts of secession, ones that had just been threats by radical Fire-Eaters in Congress, started to become more like a reality. Soon, the whole South was talking about seceding from the Union due to their discontent with the newly elected president. Believing that Lincoln and his administration posed a direct threat to slave owners, word spread quickly in the slave states that the only sensible thing to do was to leave the Union and organize as a separate country.

This sentiment was partially amplified by a speech James Buchanan gave while still serving as president. In his speech, Buchanan recognized the hostile environment in the country and stressed that the Union depended on public cooperation. He urged the two sides of the opposition to come to terms with each other since it would be the only way to preserve the unity within the country. Crucially, however, he said that if states peacefully chose to leave the Union that Congress had no constitutional right to use force to bring them back.

In a daring and shocking move, South Carolina called a state convention on December 20th, 1860, and four days later adapted the South Carolina Secession Declaration, unanimously voting to leave the Union. The authors of the declaration underlined the fact that a natural divide between the Northern and Southern states had been created. They also stressed the importance of slavery and mentioned that the North had demonstrated unjust, hostile actions against the Southern population, something which they believed was unconstitutional. An example of an unconstitutional action was the North's opposition to the Fugitive Slave Act.

Five other states—Mississippi, Florida, Georgia, Alabama, and Louisiana—followed the secession of South Carolina in January. Texas approved the decision to secede in early February and held a referendum, which also voted in favor of secession on February 23 ',

1861. Each of these states passed similar declarations, focusing on the North's unconstitutional past and the election results of 1860, which did not convey the opinion of the majority. The representatives of these states then resigned their positions in Congress and returned to their home states.

All of this happened in a time span of just two months, making it very difficult for the government, which was in the process of transitioning to a new president, to react accordingly to the situation. The truth was that secession had only been perceived as a threat before, not as something that would actually take place. There was nothing mentioned specifically on the matter of secession in the Constitution, leaving Congress unable to provide a quick and effective response. Not only that, but the supporters of secession actually believed the exact opposite, quoting the Tenth Amendment on states' rights, which says that any power that is not granted to the US federal government by the states or is not prohibited to the states by the Constitution is a right to be decided by the state in question or its people. This was a huge factor and one of the main arguments regarding the legality of the Southern states' secession from the Union.

The seceded states proceeded to meet on February 4th, 1861, in Montgomery, Alabama, a month before Lincoln's official inauguration. There, they agreed to form a new provisional government and officially formed the Confederate States of America on February 4th. The government picked Jefferson Davis, a former Mississippi representative, as president and Alexander H. Stephens of Georgia as vice president, forever changing the history of the United States.

Efforts for Reconciliation

The Confederate States of America counted seven Southern states in total by March, a number that would eventually grow to eleven by July with the states of Arkansas, Tennessee, North Carolina, and Virginia. After organizing a new government in February, they took total control of the resources present in each state, including a significant portion of the US Army, which was stationed in Texas. David E. Twiggs, a general of great experience who was in charge of the Texan army, decided to join the Confederates and became the commander of the Confederate forces.

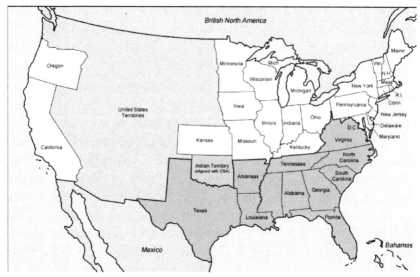

The Confederate States of America.
*Golbez, CC BY-SA 3.0 <https://creativecommons.org/licenses/by-sa/3.0>, via Wikimedia
Commons https://commons.wikimedia.org/wiki/File:CSA_1861-07-02_to_1861-10-31.png)*

We have already mentioned that the federal government's response to secession was quiet, largely due to a transitional period in Congress where Buchanan's administration was getting replaced by Lincoln. Despite the fact that some recognized the severity of the situation, only some chose to act.

One of the first efforts to avoid or solve the secession crisis was the Crittenden Compromise, a proposal by Constitutional Unionist John J. Crittenden from Kentucky. Crittenden proposed that Congress guarantee the permanent status of slavery in the United States and its territories. In addition, Crittenden included points that focused on reinstating the Missouri Compromise line, as well as a stricter Fugitive Slave Act that would be enforced in the same way throughout the country. The proposal was presented to Congress on December 18th, just two days before South Carolina unanimously voted at its state convention to leave the Union.

It is clear from first glance that the proposal would be met with fierce opposition from the Northern congressmen. Crittenden basically proposed that Congress give up all of its legislative powers to regulate slavery and give the South total control over the matter. Lincoln and his party were particularly against its passing, and since they held the majority, they killed the bill as soon as possible. The Crittenden Compromise was the final effort to satisfy the South's long-standing demands.

Nobody knows if it would have actually prevented the secession, let alone the Civil War. In hindsight, it is crucial to remember that all the measures the federal government had taken to address the issue of slavery did not provide successful long-term solutions to the problem. Thus, there is reason to believe that the Crittenden Compromise would have only caused more polarization and complicated the matter more, delaying the issue once again, just as Congress had done countless times in the past.

There were other efforts to maintain peace and unity within the Union. Former US President John Tyler, who had long been retired from politics but was concerned with the future of his country, proposed holding a special convention in Washington, DC, where representatives from both Southern and Northern states would convene and discuss the matter of secession. The representatives of all states were encouraged to attend, but the Deep South did not send any delegates, believing that the convention would not produce any important results and because they were planning to convene themselves to form a new provisional government. Thus, in total, fourteen free and seven slave states attended the convention, which was held on February 4th, just as the Montgomery convention was underway.

Now known as the Washington Peace Conference of 1861, the convention included 131 politicians who drafted a document with a similar purpose to the Crittenden Compromise. The bill aimed to reinstitute and extend the Missouri Compromise line to the Pacific Ocean and proposed to only acquire future territories with a majority vote from both the Southern and the Northern states. It also included constitutional amendments that would prevent Congress from legally interfering with the matter of slavery in the states where it existed and new, stricter laws regarding fugitive slaves.

The document drafted in Washington was almost exactly the same as the one proposed by Crittenden one and a half months before. Thus, it never saw the light of day. In the Senate, it was overwhelmingly rejected with twenty-eight votes against and only seven for.

The failed efforts to reconcile with the seceded states were followed by Abraham Lincoln's inauguration on March 4th, 1861. The whole nation awaited the president's speech, eager to find out what he would say about the Southern states that had ceased almost all contact with the North. "Legally void" is the phrase Lincoln used in his inaugural address to refer to the secession, claiming that despite the fact the states declared they had left, their decision had no effect in reality. Then, he once again repeated his stance on slavery, stating that he had never stood for abolishing slavery in the states and territories where the practice was legal but that he had always opposed its expansion in the newly acquired territories. Crucially, Lincoln underlined the fact that he would never use force to invade the South to make them rejoin the Union. However, what he did state was that he would use force against the Southern states if they seized control of the federal property located in their possessions. This included everything from mints to military forts and reserves. The president believed that he had a moral and legal obligation to do this since he had been chosen as the president of the United States by the people, binding him to all of these duties. Finally, Lincoln highlighted that he would do everything in his power to restore the "bonds which had held the Union together."

The Attack on Fort Sumter

The tensions between the two sides reached an all-time high. Even before Lincoln's inaugural address, in which he pledged to use force to defend federal property in the seceded states, both sides knew that an armed conflict was inevitable. However, neither side dared to strike first. The hostilities between South Carolina and the US Army nearly broke out at the beginning of the year over Fort Sumter, which was located at the entrance of Charleston Harbor.

At the time of South Carolina's secession, Fort Sumter was not fully finished, but it was fit to answer any threats. Instead, Fort Moultrie, a much older fort also located at the harbor, was manned. Its garrison was commanded by Major Robert Anderson. The state's authorities knew that taking control of the forts was pivotal for any sort of success in the coming conflict. They had eyed both forts since December, something that had not gone unnoticed by Anderson. He realized that if the situation got worse, he and his men would stand no chance at Moultrie. Anderson sabotaged the guns at the fort and, under cover of night, secretly moved his men to Fort Sumter on December 26th.

For the next month, Governor Francis W. Pickens engaged in fierce talks with Buchanan and his administration to order Anderson and his men to surrender Fort Sumter to South Carolina, claiming that the existence of an armed fort by hostile forces was harmful to the state's security. Buchanan responded that Fort Sumter was the property of the United States government and that Major Anderson was entitled to move his forces from one US Army fort to another. This infuriated Governor Pickens, who ordered state troops to proceed with seizing all other federal assets in South Carolina. His men also made sure that no one went in or out of the fort, depriving those in Fort Sumter of supplies. At the end of January, Governor Pickens once again contacted President Buchanan and demanded the fort's surrender. He received a negative response.

The tensions between the men at Fort Sumter and the South Carolina secessionists would not escalate for another four months. Lincoln's administration was aware of the pressing situation and was working on a solution. If the crisis in Charleston was not enough, a similar situation was happening in Fort Pickens in Florida, where Union men were surrounded by hostile secessionists. Lincoln was reluctant to act first, realizing that he might have been considered the aggressor, something that would have had negative implications for his presidency. In Lincoln's Cabinet, William H. Seward, who had now assumed the position of secretary of state, advised the president to order the troops to retreat, but Lincoln disagreed.

On the other side of the border, where the Confederate States of America had already been established, Confederate President Davis was in the same dilemma as his counterpart, acknowledging the fact that taking the fort was crucial but that acting first was not an option. A delegation from the South visited Washington with an offer to buy all the federal property in the seceded lands and to make peace with the Union, but Lincoln denied the delegates, stating that engaging in any sort of negotiations would mean that he acknowledged that the Confederacy was a sovereign nation, something that was unacceptable to him.

By early April, Fort Sumter had almost completely run out of supplies, but the spirits among the men in the fort were still relatively high. Anderson had eighty-five soldiers who could fight but about fifty or so other noncombatant men with him, making the situation even worse. Lincoln was aware of this and communicated with Pickens on April 6th, telling him that a relief ship with no soldiers or ammunition would deliver food and other necessary supplies to Fort Sumter. Crucially, Lincoln made contact with Pickens as the US governor of South Carolina, not the Confederate provisional government. This move is recognized to be perhaps the first of Lincoln's many diplomatic triumphs during the course of the Civil War.

Lincoln's message was discussed by President Davis and his advisors. After much consideration, a crucial decision was made, despite some opposition from Davis's cabinet. Davis ordered the commander of the Confederate forces in South Carolina—Pierre "P. G. T." Beauregard—to once again demand the surrender of Fort Sumter. In the event of a negative response, Beauregard was to proceed with an assault on the fort before the supply ship got to it.

Early in the morning of April 12th, the first shot of the Civil War was fired on Fort Sumter, the first out of four thousand upon the fort. Anderson and his men, who were outgunned and outnumbered, knew the end was near but still put up a fight. Fort Sumter fell the next day, with no casualties on either side. Anderson was forced to agree to surrender as it was a desperate situation.

The North grieved the loss of Fort Sumter, and everyone was waiting for Lincoln's response. On April 15th, two days after the fort's surrender, Lincoln named the secession of the Southern states an "insurrection." In addition, he called all states to assemble a voluntary force consisting of seventy-five thousand men to serve for three months, a decisive action that rallied the public and concentrated their efforts. Volunteers enlisted by the thousands, quickly meeting the president's demands, and prepared for an armed conflict. America was now at war, but it was at war with itself.

Border States

Despite the fact that the attention of Congress and Lincoln's administration was divided between trying to come up with a plan to reconcile with the South and dealing with the crisis of Fort Sumter, other important issues remained. One very important question that needed to be answered was what would happen to the slave states that had not yet chosen to secede from the Union. During the attack on Fort Sumter, the Confederate States of America still consisted of the Deep Seven. However, there were eight other slave states that still had to make their decisions.

These states were divided on the matter. Half of these states made their decisions soon after Lincoln's actions regarding Fort Sumter. Beginning in May 1861, Virginia, Arkansas, Tennessee, and North Carolina all seceded from the Union and were accepted by the Confederacy. The population of these states was heavily dependent on slavery and saw the election of Lincoln and the Republicans as a direct threat to their everyday lives.

The other four states—Maryland, Delaware, Kentucky, and Missouri—were more hesitant. Although slavery was allowed in these states, the public was much less one-sided. Instead of choosing to remain or secede, these states left it to the public to decide what they wanted. As a consequence, Maryland, Delaware, Kentucky, and Missouri have come to be known as border states since none of them seceded from the Union but existed in a weird symbiotic relationship with both the North and the South.

In Missouri, a state convention was assembled on whether to hold a referendum, a decision much like the one that had been taken in Texas. Unlike Texas, the referendum demonstrated overwhelming support for remaining with the Union.

Maryland, whose territories surrounded Washington, DC, was in a much trickier situation. Despite its proximity to the capital, there was more support for secession. But giving up Maryland to the Confederacy would mean that the war effort would come knocking right at the door of the Union's capital, and Lincoln was not prepared enough for that kind of pressure. Maryland's legislature voted in favor of remaining with the Union, but the same resolution also mentioned that it would not get involved in the war, shutting down the crucial railroads that connected the North with the South. Lincoln responded by declaring martial law and making sure that all anti-Union officials and members of the Maryland General Assembly were arrested. His troops then quickly took control of the state. During the war and after its completion, Lincoln would be criticized for his actions, which some have deemed to be dictatorial or undemocratic.

In Delaware, things were decided in a much easier way. Despite the fact that slavery was permitted, the state was hardly reliant on it. Since 1860, the North had made quite an effort in trying to integrate Delaware's economy into its own. The general assembly opposed secession. The general public sentiment also reflected this decision, as average citizens were not slave owners and would rather see the conflict end through peaceful means. The fact that Delaware was deep into Northern territory also may have influenced the decision since it would have been much harder for the Confederacy to defend Delaware.

The situation proved to be the most explosive in Kentucky. Several different opinions existed on what exactly to do, but the state finally passed the legislation on assuming neutrality in May, declaring that it would continue to be neutral if neither side invaded it. Throughout the course of the war, both the Union and the Confederacy saw Kentucky as one of their own, and Kentuckians enlisted in both armies. After the Unionists gained additional seats in the state election in the summer of 1861, the Confederacy was only supported by a small minority of state officials. The Confederate forces did invade Kentucky but were met with fierce opposition from the Unionists, who did not give an inch to the invaders and managed to cling onto the most valuable parts of the state, including its capital, Frankfort. Throughout the war, the Confederacy recognized Kentucky as one of the Confederate states and even included it in the final version of the flag. President Lincoln personally noted on different occasions just how pivotal holding Kentucky was for the Union and the defensive effort in the war.

Chapter 7 – America at War

Now that we have covered the preluding events of the Civil War, it is time to jump right into the action. This chapter will focus on examining the strengths and weaknesses of the Union and the Confederacy throughout the Civil War and cover some of the main strategies each side employed.

Was the US Prepared for War?

Despite the fact that the United States had yet to be defeated in a foreign war after gaining independence, it is safe to say when looking at the country's military resources in the 1860s that it was *not* prepared for war, let alone a war with itself. It had a standing military of about sixteen thousand soldiers—a tiny number when compared to the great empires of Europe in the 19ᵗʰ century. Yet, in 1812, the United States had managed to hold off the British, and in the 1840s, it had decisively defeated Mexico, despite the fact that the Mexican Army far outnumbered the US Army. So, where exactly did their secret lie?

The sixteen thousand men already ready for service were dispersed around the country in small numbers; Major Anderson and his soldiers at Fort Sumter are just one example. They were stationed everywhere, from fortified Native American territories to the harbors. The Founding Fathers had based the country's military philosophy on mustering up militias when there was a need for them during wartime. The militia system was based solely on voluntary service; states would supply men who wanted to fight. After the end of the war, these men would normally disperse, returning back to their lives, if possible, with only a minority continuing formal training and service.

On paper, the North was far more capable militarily than the South. More than twice the number of Southerners lived in the North, and about half of the Southerners were slaves. This gave the Union a significant edge manpower-wise. In a long, dragged-out war of attrition, it theoretically could have relied on this edge to achieve victory. And due to the South's reliance on the agrarian lifestyle and slavery, the North had far more industrial capabilities to produce weapons. Fewer than 20,000 manufacturing plants were located south of the Potomac River, while the North had about 100,000 at its disposal.

Despite this apparent disadvantage, the Confederacy hoped to put up a good fight, banking on the possibility of foreign aid from Europe, mainly from France and Britain. Engaging in what has come to be known as cotton diplomacy, the Confederate government requested aid from the Europeans and threatened to block cotton exports as a leverage factor. However, partially thanks to the efforts of Secretary of State Seward, who duly notified the Europeans that recognizing the Confederacy would mean antagonizing the Union government, and partially due to the fact that the Europeans could get their cotton from Asia, cotton diplomacy failed. Confederate President Davis and his government were perhaps too hopeful that Europe would interfere in the war and were disappointed when they learned they would be alone.

Although the Confederacy was outgunned and outmanned against the Union, the Confederates had high morale. They were united around the infamous "Southern cause," a notion that the Southerners had to achieve victory against the tyrannical North, which tried to limit the sacred Southern institutions, most importantly slavery. It was a typical narrative of David versus Goliath, with David, in this case, being the Confederacy. This idea had existed in the South before the start of the war but was amplified to higher degrees throughout the war by Confederate politicians.

What is important to realize is that the two sides had chosen completely different approaches to the war. This became more evident as the war entered its first stages. Davis and the Confederates knew they were at a numerical disadvantage and chose a more defensive tactic. Davis hoped the long southern coastline would make it impossible for the Union to completely blockade the South. A slower approach guaranteed that the Confederates would be able to defend their territories more cohesively and not be distracted by an offensive and find themselves at a disadvantage.

Some historians argue that the decision to adopt a defensive approach might have been fatal for the Confederates from the very beginning. Immediately after the events at Fort Sumter, it might have been better to organize a concentrated attack on the Union's positions when the North would have least expected it and, therefore, might have been less prepared. When paired with the dragged-out approach adopted by Lincoln and his team, this move seems more logical.

In what is referred to as the Anaconda Plan, the Northern high command envisioned the defeat of the Confederacy by a complete naval and land blockade of the South, followed by a concentrated attack along the Mississippi River—right at the heart of the South.

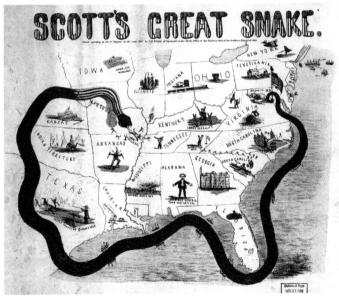

The Anaconda Plan.
https://commons.wikimedia.org/wiki/File:Scott-anaconda.jpg

The Fight for West Virginia

The attack on Fort Sumter was a cold shower for the Union and contributed to the growth of anti-Southern (or rather anti-secessionist) sentiment, which had existed in the country since December 1860. Out of the sixteen thousand or so soldiers in the army, more than half of them were located in the western part of the country at the time of the attack. It seemed unlikely that they would join up with the seventy-five thousand or so volunteers President Lincoln had called upon from the Northern states. Still, before the mustering of volunteers was completed, fighting between the Union and Confederate troops broke out in early June. The Union forces attempted to take control of the western part of Virginia, which was more pro-Union than the rest of the slave state.

Virginia had seceded from the Union in May and had been admitted by the Confederacy on May 7th. At the time, about 30 percent of its population were slaves, but they, along with the majority of slave owners, were concentrated in the eastern part of the state. In the west, pro-Unionists were discontent with the decision to secede from the Union. To use the situation to the Union's favor, Major General George B. McClellan, who was the leader of the assembled Union forces in Cincinnati, Ohio, marched to western Virginia with a pretty sizeable force of about twenty thousand men. His opposition was not ready. Confederate Colonel George A. Porterfield was in charge of the Confederate force stationed in northwestern Virginia but was not aware that an attack was imminent.

In what became the first land battle of the American Civil War, McClellan's three thousand or so men converged on the town of Philippi. They were able to rout a much smaller Confederate force of about eight hundred men, forcing them to retreat south to the town of Huttonsville. The whole encounter was more of a skirmish rather than an all-out battle, but it still counted as a victory for the Union Army, which was able to establish a somewhat favorable position in western Virginia. There were only about thirty casualties in total, but Philippi was almost completely destroyed after hours of shelling by the Union forces.

After the triumph at Philippi, McClellan and his men were praised by Northern newspapers for their bravery. McClellan was able to follow this up with two additional victories in western Virginia. A month later, at the Battle of Rich Mountain, McClellan's forces were able to inflict about three hundred casualties to the Confederate forces while suffering only forty themselves. They chased down the retreating opposition to Carrick's Ford, where they also emerged victorious, concluding the first set of battles fought in Virginia.

McClellan's efforts were quickly recognized by the Union high command, and his three quick victories were a factor behind his promotion to commander of the Army of the Potomac. The success of the Union forces was also crucial in the secession of pro-Union Virginians from their state. The anti-slavery state of West Virginia eventually separated from Virginia and aided the Union throughout the war.

The First Battle of Bull Run

An interesting characteristic of the war is that the capitals of the two sides—Washington for the Union and Richmond for the Confederacy—were very close to each other, separated by only about one hundred miles. Richmond was one of the richest and most prosperous Southern cities, so the Confederates chose to move their capital to the city after Virginia joined the Confederacy on May 7th. Because of this rather unusual situation, the tensions surrounding both sides started circulating early on. The largest parts of both armies were gathering near Washington and Richmond, and the cities' inhabitants sensed that, sooner or later, they would be under attack.

Union Brigadier General Irvin McDowell was in charge of the thirty-five thousand volunteers who had assembled at Washington. Despite the fact that the Anaconda Plan had been proposed by US General in Chief Winfield Scott, McDowell was tasked to lead the attack on enemy positions. The Confederates, who were commanded by P. G. T. Beauregard, had encamped about twenty-six miles south from Washington at the pivotal Manassas Junction, which played an important role in terms of rail connectivity to the east. Beauregard was in charge of about twenty thousand men and assumed a defensive position at Manassas. In addition, a smaller Confederate force of about twelve thousand men was encamped nearby, ready to reinforce in case of emergency.

On July 21ˢᵗ, McDowell, knowing that he had a numerical advantage over the enemy and succumbing to the social and political pressure in Washington, led his men against Beauregard. An additional force of eighteen thousand men commanded by Major General Robert Patterson was tasked to delay the reinforcements at Harpers Ferry.

Initially, McDowell's troops saw great success, managing to outmaneuver the enemy and weaken its left flank. However, the upper hand was quickly assumed by the Confederates, thanks to an inspiring rally from Thomas "Stonewall" Jackson—a Confederate general who earned his nickname due to this battle. Despite experiencing heavy artillery fire, Beauregard's men were able to contain McDowell, while the Confederate reinforcements, which had managed to break through Patterson's resistance, arrived just in time to outflank the Union Army. Union volunteers, who had relatively low morale because of inexperience, decided to flee and save their lives. McDowell was forced to retreat back to Washington, causing a city-wide panic because of his defeat.

The encounter became known as the First Battle of Bull Run in the North, while the Southerners referred to it as the Battle of First Manassas. It was a tough defeat to swallow for the North, which lost about 2,900 men compared to the South's 2,000. Fortunately for the Union, Beauregard's men were too exhausted to chase the retreating soldiers. Thus, the two sides interpreted the battle's outcome differently.

After the loss, the Union approach became more careful instead of assuming a proactive role and using its numerical advantage to the fullest to overwhelm the enemy forces. As for the South, the situation was not that different. The Confederacy saw the victory as hard proof that despite a numerical disadvantage, the Southern soldiers were more resilient than the Northerners. They were swept up in the idea that the "Southern cause" was far more important than what the Union was fighting for, giving them a natural advantage over their enemy and, as a consequence, making them overestimate their own capabilities.

Army of the Potomac

The defeat at the First Battle of Bull Run was devastating for Lincoln, who had hoped for a decisive action by the end of July but had only gotten a relatively small victory in western Virginia. As he called for more volunteers to bolster the army's numbers and replenish the loss the Union had suffered, he also made changes to the high command. General Winfield Scott, the long-standing general in chief, was replaced in November by Major General McClellan, who earned his spot due to his quick victories over the summer. Although the overall plans laid by Scott remained intact, the experienced veteran had to be relieved due to his poor health.

Just five days after the Union's defeat at Manassas, McClellan started the transformation of his corps into the Army of the Potomac, the part of the Union Army during the Civil War that would take part in the military operations in the eastern campaigns. In the first months as the new general in chief, the number of volunteers grew to include more than 100,000 men, who, unlike the troops that participated in the First Battle of Bull Run, were substantially drilled and equipped. McClellan's main goal was to raise discipline, which would allow for more resilience on the battlefield.

Despite this, McClellan still faced some opposition from the Republican-dominated Congress, partially due to the fact that he was a Democrat. Congress was aware of the enemy's close proximity, as they had not only remained in Manassas but also occupied the territory near the town of Centreville, Virginia. In addition to having a bad reputation with Congress for sometimes demonstrating impolite and indelicate tendencies, McClellan also found himself in a personal feud with President Lincoln. After McClellan recovered from an illness in late January 1861, Lincoln ordered him to organize an attack on the Confederate positions in Virginia. McClellan disagreed, believing that the volunteers were still not fit for battle, despite the fact that they had greatly improved their capabilities after his arrival. Still, Lincoln's decision was final, and McClellan was obliged to advance on the enemy in late February.

Chapter 8 – The War Grows

In the beginning, many in the North predicted the conflict would last no more than a couple of months. This was especially true after McClellan's early victories in western Virginia. However, by the end of 1861, as substantial efforts to put a dent into the Confederacy's defense proved unsuccessful, the approach from both the North and the South drastically changed.

The Peninsular Campaign

Acting on orders from the upper chain of command, Union General in Chief McClellan led his men in yet another offensive. In February, President Lincoln's main concern was the Confederate Army stationed at Centreville, Virginia, about thirty miles south of Washington. The president had perhaps overestimated the threat the Confederate forces could have posed to the Union's capital, which was heavily defended and contained a sizeable garrison.

At first, Lincoln ordered McClellan to attack Centreville. However, before the operation could be started, the Confederates retreated farther south, deeming the attack useless. Instead, McClellan's attention was focused on the Confederate capital of Richmond. McClellan finally managed to gain Lincoln's approval for an offensive after proposing to organize an attack from the East Coast by first landing at Fort Monroe through an amphibious assault and then marching his troops northeastward, all the way up the Virginia Peninsula to finally reach Richmond.

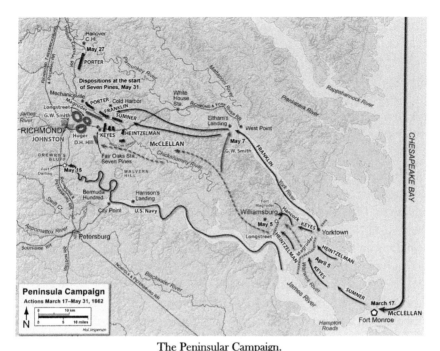

The Peninsular Campaign.

Hlj, CC BY-SA 4.0 <https://creativecommons.org/licenses/by-sa/4.0>, via Wikimedia Commons, https://commons.wikimedia.org/wiki/File:Peninsula_Campaign_March-May_1862.png

Despite the soundness of the plan, nothing went as smoothly as the Union high command had desired. One big detail to remember is that McClellan was relieved from the position of general in chief once the operation started, partially because of his feud with Lincoln and the Republicans but also because Lincoln hoped he could divert his whole attention to leading his campaign. President Lincoln assumed the position of general in chief and, together with his Cabinet, personally led the war effort until he could find a suitable replacement.

As for the Peninsular Campaign itself, the initial plans to land at Fort Monroe and converge on the town of Yorktown, both from the land and from the York River, failed. The Union forces faced several delays and were even confronted by Confederate vanguards in smaller skirmishes that cost them days. Finally, McClellan's troops reached the city. After a long siege, they forced the Confederates to give up their positions in early May.

Confederate Commander Joseph E. Johnston fell back to a more defensive line at Williamsburg, but McClellan quickly caught up and forced another confrontation, where the Union soldiers emerged victorious once again. Finally, after breaking through the defensive lines under tough conditions, McClellan found himself a target for a Confederate counterattack at the Battle of Seven Pines. There, Commander Johnston hoped to isolate McClellan's flank and surround the advancing Union forces. But after gaining a small advantage at first, he was forced to fall back, succumbing to the superior Union artillery.

The final outcome at Seven Pines favored neither side. The Confederate resistance had significantly slowed McClellan's momentum, who was forced to take a break before continuing his advance. On the other hand, Johnston was wounded during the battle and replaced by General Robert E. Lee—a man who had been serving as a military advisor to Jefferson Davis before stepping up to take control of the Confederate Army of Northern Virginia. In the long run, both outcomes proved to be terrible for the Union since Lee proved to be its toughest opponent in the war and greatly slowed the initiative that had been seized by McClellan during the Peninsular Campaign.

By the end of June, McClellan's forces had made headway into the Confederate territories. At the same time, fighting was unfolding in western parts of Virginia, mainly in the Shenandoah Valley, where Union corps under the command of Major General McDowell tried to converge on Richmond. However, the Confederates fiercely defended themselves against the Union troops that tried to cross the Potomac River. The Confederates gained several victories and seized a lot of valuable loot, like small arms and ammunition, in the battles of Front Royal and Winchester. Since the Confederates had thwarted the Union advance in the Shenandoah Valley, Stonewall Jackson, who was in command of the defending troops, turned his attention to the east to reinforce Lee.

This decision turned out to be crucial. Lee waited for almost a month for McClellan to attack. So, in the meantime, he gathered up his defenses in the southern and southeastern parts of Richmond and was ready to put up a fight with an additional couple of thousand soldiers. He organized a counterattack on June 26th, trying to further stall out McClellan's advance and make the Union forces run out of supplies so they would be forced to retreat. The ensuing battles lasted for about a week and are referred to as the Seven Days

Battles. In a well-organized, concentrated assault, Lee was able to utilize the surprise factor and achieved victory after victory. He first pushed the Union forces back at Mechanicsville and at Gaines' Mill on June 26th and 27th, which was followed by another set of victories at Savage's Station and Frayser's Farm by June 30th and Glendale and Malvern Hill by July 1st. Lee was able to reclaim a lot of lost ground.

Lee was proudly celebrated in the South, while the Northern high command was furious with McClellan, who they believed had thrown away the advantage they had achieved. In hindsight, it was a rather peculiar situation since, despite suffering some defeats, McClellan was still somewhat close to Richmond. Who knows, perhaps with more effort and reinforcements, he could have been able to reach the Confederate capital, but this was not something that neither he nor the high command believed to be feasible.

The truth of the matter is that McClellan already had an infamous reputation in the Union, and the fact that he requested more reinforcements to continue the campaign was perceived as another one of his unrealistic demands. In total, McClellan had lost more than fifteen thousand men throughout the campaign, while Lee had suffered about twenty thousand casualties. Although McClellan's early efforts had been successful, Lee had retaliated. Lee still had a lot to prove on the battlefield, and the war was nowhere near over. Instead of continuing the advance up the peninsula, Lincoln ordered a retreat to consolidate the forces and plan a new attack.

The Second Battle of Bull Run

After the unsuccessful Peninsular Campaign, Lincoln appointed Henry W. Halleck to the position of general in chief, which had been left open for months. McClellan was still the commander of the Army of the Potomac, but many of his troops eventually ended up under the command of John Pope in the newly formed Army of Virginia. The main idea behind the Army of Virginia was to have an additional force Lincoln could rely on, as McClellan had proven to be increasingly difficult to work with. Instead of attempting to recreate the previous offensive from the east, Pope's forces would try to converge on Richmond from the north and west.

Confederate Commander Lee envisioned a different development of the war. Although McClellan was still on the peninsula, Lee had become aware of his dwindling reputation among the members of the high command and decided to allocate fewer resources to keep his forces at bay. He recognized that Pope's Army of Virginia, which was marching to Gordonsville to start a new offensive on Richmond, had completely split from McClellan, who was on the other side of Virginia. Lee wanted to seize the opportunity and quickly strike Pope's position, hoping to take him out with a concentrated attack that would leave the Union even more disoriented.

With this in mind, he sent Stonewall Jackson with about fourteen thousand men to stop Pope at Gordonsville before the two Union armies could join up. He planned to follow up with even more reinforcements to crush Pope's forces. The initial plan worked. Stonewall Jackson was able to contain most of Pope's forces at Manassas, near the site of the original Battle of Bull Run, forcing Pope to make an aggressive move without waiting for more reinforcements.

In late August, Pope engaged with Jackson's forces in what has come to be known as the Second Battle of Bull Run but could not achieve a significant advantage, as Stonewall Jackson lived up to his reputation as a great defender. After holding off the Union Army, Jackson's job was done, and Lee, along with Confederate Brigadier General James Longstreet, arrived just in time to flank Pope. They routed his men, inflicting more than thirteen thousand casualties while, in turn, suffering only about nine thousand.

Invasion of Maryland

Having gained several consecutive victories, first against McClellan in June and then against Pope in August, Lee was determined to achieve more. This time, he planned to go on a full offensive and use the momentum to push his success by invading Maryland—a border state where Lincoln had declared martial law to enforce order and subdue anti-Republican tendencies. Lee hoped to achieve several victories in Maryland to motivate it to join the Confederacy, something that would have been detrimental to the Union. If Maryland joined the Confederacy, the security of

Washington, DC, would come under question. Capturing the pivotal Baltimore and Ohio Railroad would also cut off a major supply line to the Union capital.

After learning of Lee's advance to Frederick, Maryland, Lincoln desperately thought of an effective answer as he slowly noticed panic build up within the Northern public. McClellan's operation from the peninsula had been fully recalled, with Lincoln tasking him with coming up with a response. Having finally joined up with the rest of Pope's troops, McClellan did what he did best: make sure that his men were fully capable of fighting and reconsolidated his position. However, he also demonstrated his main weakness once again: he was too hesitant to take decisive action against Lee because he overestimated the South's military capabilities.

This became even more evident when McClellan was notified of Lee's future plans after his men accidentally found a Confederate piece of paper that depicted the intended campaign. Instead of utilizing the element of surprise and picking off the smaller Confederate forces one by one, McClellan decided to wait for nearly a day and only managed to confront a larger Confederate force that had assembled at South Mountain on September 14th, 1862. There, after some skirmishes, Lee ordered his men to retreat to assume a more favorable defensive position at Antietam Creek near Sharpsburg, where he awaited a Union attack.

Robert E. Lee
https://commons.wikimedia.org/wiki/File:Robert_Edward_Lee.jpg

At Antietam Creek, Lee was joined by Stonewall Jackson's reinforcements, and the two Confederate commanders, along with General Longstreet, put up one of the best defensive efforts of the whole war. Antietam Creek was a rather irregular location to attack and gave the defenders an advantage, as they could use the small rivers to their favor. Nevertheless, a long front line was established, and early on September 17th, McClellan ordered his men to attack. Most of the fighting took place in the center at an area called "Bloody Road," where McClellan's forces broke through. However, Confederate reinforcements from the flanks, where less of the action was concentrated, quickly moved to the center to drive the Union forces back to their original front lines.

Crucially, additional reinforcements arrived at the same time for both armies, further contributing to the deadlock that had been created after hours of fighting. A deciding factor in the battle was, once again, McClellan's indecisiveness. The Union commander wrongly assumed the Confederates' strength and was reluctant to send in all of his soldiers to overwhelm the defenders despite having the numerical advantage. Lee and the Confederates, on the other hand, had been fully committed to the battle and fought until they were forced to retreat after realizing they did not stand a chance in a prolonged confrontation.

About twenty-three thousand men fell at the Battle of Antietam, which earned its infamous status as the single bloodiest day of the Civil War. The Confederates lost a bit more than ten thousand men, while the Union suffered about thirteen thousand casualties. However, these numbers are even more impressive when considering the fact that McClellan's forces outnumbered Lee's army two to one, coming in at about eighty-five thousand men to Lee's thirty-six thousand. Despite the Confederate retreat, the Union was not fully able to capitalize due to McClellan's distorted perception of the South's strength. Still, the Confederate offensive into Maryland was over, and Lee's main army was driven back to Virginia.

Fiasco at Fredericksburg

Although most of the Confederate forces had managed to retreat, Antietam was perceived by the Union high command as a victory. For the next few weeks after the end of the battle, Lincoln and his war council repeatedly urged McClellan to pursue the retreating Confederates, but the latter always refused, stating he was afraid to overextend his men and unwilling to chase Lee since he did not know his full strength. This back-and-forth lasted until the end of October. President Lincoln finally relieved McClellan of his duties as the commander of the Army of the Potomac and assigned Ambrose E. Burnside as the new leader. He had previously been in charge of one of the companies at Antietam but failed to achieve anything meaningful throughout the course of the battle. The Union high command was hoping to at least have someone whom they could rely on to follow their orders.

This approach from Lincoln and his Cabinet worked, and Burnside launched a follow-up offensive aimed to make an advance straight to Richmond. His freshly reinforced army counted some 120,000 men. Theoretically, it was designed to overcome any resistance the South could dish up simply because of its numerical superiority. Burnside's plan envisioned a quick crossing of the Rappahannock River and outmaneuvering Lee's army to get to the relatively undefended Confederate capital. At first, it seemed as if the plan was going to work, but Burnside's army was delayed for weeks because the special pontoon bridges—the ones that float on water and are used by armies to quickly cross rivers—did not arrive due to logistical issues. This delay gave Lee and his men time to encamp on the other bank of the Rappahannock and set up defenses near the town of Fredericksburg.

Battle of Fredericksburg.
https://commons.wikimedia.org/wiki/File:Battle_of_Fredericksburg,_Dec_13,_1862.png

Pressured by the Union high command, Burnside proceeded to establish crossing points and crossed the river to the other bank, where Lee and his men were waiting with heavy artillery fire, having assumed the high ground on the nearby heights south of the city. However, if there is one thing military history has clearly demonstrated is that the defenders are always favored during river crossings. Burnside ordered his men to head right into the open arms of the Confederates, who were more than happy to pick off waves after waves of hopeless Union soldiers. On December 15th, 1862, after about five days of fighting, Burnside realized that he had made a fatal mistake. He ordered his men to retreat back across the Rappahannock River and accepted defeat.

The loss at Fredericksburg was detrimental to the Union Army's morale. The army suffered about thirteen thousand casualties to the Confederates' five thousand, marking one of the most decisive Union defeats in the war. And to add insult to injury, Burnside suffered another fiasco in the weeks following the Battle of Fredericksburg during a desperate flanking maneuver on Lee's forces.

In harsh winter conditions and lacking effective communication channels, Burnside was not able to achieve his goals for the whole of January, seeing a rising number of desertions and a lack of trust from the commanders directly under him. This caused President Lincoln to relieve Burnside from the position of the commander of the Army of the Potomac on January 25th, 1863, replacing him with the more experienced Joseph "Fighting Joe" Hooker. The two sides went into a temporary stalemate over the winter of 1863.

The Emancipation Proclamation

Ironically enough, the Union's lack of success on the battlefield was completely different from the crucial developments of late 1862 and early 1863 off the field. The instrumental Emancipation Proclamation—one of the most iconic documents in the history of the United States—was signed on January 1st, 1863, by President Lincoln, declaring all slaves living in seceded states to be freed. The signing of the Emancipation Proclamation was not only a huge social and moral victory for Lincoln and the Union but also a great strategic move.

The slavery issue became even more pressing for both sides. The Confederacy was dependent on slave labor, which was the main catalyst of its economy. The Union, on the other hand, had seen a vast increase in the number of fugitive slaves who had escaped from the South, seeking shelter and safety, afraid that with the secession of the Southern states, their chances of gaining freedom were non-existent. This factor, in addition to Southern reliance on slavery, was recognized by President Lincoln, but he was still hesitant to issue an emancipation bill or abolish the practice altogether. Mainly, Lincoln was afraid that in case of emancipation, the instrumental slave-owning border states might rebel against the Union and join the Confederacy. Slaves were also considered the property of their owners and thus were protected by the Constitution, something that would have been very difficult to change.

However, with Congress passing the First Confiscation Act in August of 1861, allowing Union soldiers to confiscate the property of the Confederate soldiers, the margins on the right to property, as mentioned in the Constitution, became thinner. In other words, with the First Confiscation Act, the Union troops were permitted to claim the slaves who had previously been in the defeated Confederates' possession.

The Union soldiers liberated hundreds of slaves throughout the course of the first two years. It put a dent into the South's production. With the majority of white Confederates enlisted in the army, every slave who would do the work for them in factories and fields mattered even more than before. Famously, Union General and politician Benjamin F. Butler referred to the slaves that would be seized during the campaigns as "contrabands," declaring that they would not be returned to their previous owners under any circumstances. The name stuck, and for the rest of the war, the escaped slaves were increasingly referred to as contrabands.

The First Confiscation Act and the increased number of fugitive slaves prompted Congress to abolish slavery in the District of Columbia in April 1862. The slave owners in the area received monetary compensation for the income they would lose. Still, DC was the easiest place to negotiate emancipation, followed by the US territories.

The situation was not quite as simple when it came to the border states, whose representatives met Lincoln on separate occasions to discuss the terms of potential emancipation. Lincoln offered monetary compensation to the slave owners of Missouri, Kentucky, Maryland, and Delaware but to no real success. These states had largely operated on their own since the start of the war, and Lincoln had to get them on board before he could make such an impactful decision. As the talks fell through, Lincoln was forced to draft a new version of the Emancipation Proclamation, which would eventually take effect from January 1st, 1863. The proclamation stated that starting in the new year, all slaves in the territories not under the control of the Union were free.

It was a monumental step for Lincoln and his administration, something that would not only give the moral high ground to the North but also incentivize slaves living in oppression in the South to break free from their owners and cause further harm to the South's economy. Crucially, Lincoln had used smart wording to indicate that the Emancipation Proclamation did not include the border states since they were still technically under the Union's control. It only affected the states that had seceded, where the practice of slavery was the most deeply rooted.

The Emancipation Proclamation was declared right after the Battle of Antietam. Despite mixed results, it was conceived by the Union high command as a victory. The implications of the Emancipation Proclamation were huge, and everyone waited for January to see what effect it would have on the slave population of the South. Historians note that the signing of the Emancipation Proclamation was one of the reasons behind Europe's decision not to support the Confederacy against the Union. The practice of slavery was frowned upon by the major powers of Europe at this time.

The immediate effects of the Emancipation Proclamation are evident. One important point of the document was that freed slaves and already freed African Americans could now serve as soldiers in the war on the side of the Union. Before 1863, African Americans and whites were not allowed to serve together in the US Army or Navy, although they were permitted to join the ranks in emergency situations like in the War of 1812. In total, about 200,000 black soldiers entered the war on the side of the Union, twenty thousand of whom joined the navy. They made up approximately 10 percent of all Union forces by the end of the war, and many of them had escaped their Southern masters to fight, just as Lincoln had envisioned.

The role played by African Americans in the Civil War is truly immense. They were instrumental in the battles that occurred as the Northern effort became more concentrated down the Mississippi, in Louisiana, and in South Carolina. It must have been a great sight to see those who had struggled for so long for their liberty to finally have a realistic chance to fight for it. Still, despite joining the Union Army in large numbers, the African Americans could not escape segregation, which they had faced all their lives. They were paid less than their white counterparts, were organized in separate "all-black" regiments, and had limited direct contact with white leadership. Their regiments were commanded by white officers since they rarely ascended in the ranks. The sense of "Negrophobia" that had always characterized Northern society showed itself once African Americans poured into the army. Although they were fighting for the same cause, the Northern soldiers' innate racism was something the African Americans had to bear with for the rest of the war.

The Trans-Mississippi

Along with the Eastern Theater of the Civil War, which historians refer to as the military action that unfolded mainly in Virginia and the surrounding areas, fighting between the Union and the Confederates took place in other parts of the country, one of which was the Trans-Mississippi Theater, where the war effort was more disorganized than in the east.

Several small-scale skirmishes and guerilla warfare were already present in the region, which spanned the territories west of the Mississippi River, mainly in the states of Missouri, Arkansas, Louisiana, and modern-day Oklahoma. It is important to remember that at the beginning of the war, both sides were quite unsure of the main goals set by their respective high commands. Thus, the fighting took place mainly to test and weaken the opposition rather than to have a decisive effect.

A more cohesive campaign in the Trans-Mississippi was organized by Confederate Commander Henry Sibley, who led his force of around 3,5000 men to New Mexico and managed to capture the cities of Albuquerque and Santa Fe by late March 1862. Sibley's intended objective was to reach California, as the control of the rich state would give many opportunities to the Confederate government. However, Sibley was forced to retreat back to Texas with heavy casualties after he was confronted by Edward Canby at the Battle of La Glorieta Pass.

Meanwhile, more concentrated encounters had taken place in the border states northeast of New Mexico. President Lincoln was well aware of the important role the border states, especially Kentucky and Missouri, played in the war and was prepared to divert most of his resources to defend the territories. At the first major battle between the two sides at Wilson's Creek, Missouri, around five thousand Union soldiers suffered a defeat against a much larger Confederate force, which managed to briefly seize control of the southern part of the state in August 1861. The North, however, was not willing to give up Missouri without a proper fight. After reinforcing the numbers under Brigadier General Samuel R.

Curtis, the Union dealt a decisive blow to the Confederates at the Battle of Pea Ridge in March 1862. Before March 1862, neither side had the resources necessary to continue fighting in Missouri, as most actions at the time were taking place in Virginia due to the attempted Northern campaign to capture Richmond.

Farther east in Kentucky, fighting broke out when the Confederates violated the state's neutrality, assuming a commanding position by capturing Columbus. Led by General Albert Sidney Johnston, the Confederates convinced the anti-Union population of Kentucky to secede from the state and organized a provisional government, which admitted Kentucky into the Confederacy in December 1861. However, the long front line the Confederates had established proved to be difficult to maintain since they simply did not have enough manpower. Seizing the opportunity, the Union forces were able to break through, first at Mill Springs on the right flank of the Confederate line in January and then at Fort Henry and Fort Donelson in the center about a month later. By capturing these two important forts, the Union had virtually gained control of the Cumberland River, which was the main point of defense for the Confederates.

The Union forces under Ulysses S. Grant were able to drive the Confederates out of both Kentucky and northern Tennessee, suffering only about three thousand casualties while inflicting more than fifteen thousand to the enemy. The battles at Fort Henry and Fort Donelson are considered to be the first meaningful victories of the Union in the war, despite the fact that in the Virginia Theater, McClellan and others had seen some successes before this.

Ulysses S. Grant
https://commons.wikimedia.org/wiki/File:Ulysses_S._Grant_1870-1880.jpg

By the end of March 1862, Confederate General Johnston had given up his positions in Kentucky and retreated back to Tennessee to regroup, awaiting a new opportunity to strike. This opportunity presented itself to Johnston early in April when the Union forces under Ulysses S. Grant and William Tecumseh Sherman decided to capitalize on their previous victories and advance over the Tennessee River. They knew that reinforcements under Don Carlos Buell would soon arrive from Nashville, where they had seen little resistance and had captured the Tennessean capital. However, as it turned out, Grant was walking right into Johnston's trap.

At the Battle of Shiloh, which started on April 6th, a Confederate force of about forty thousand troops ambushed Grant and the Union forces, driving them back by nightfall. Although Johnston hoped to have crushed Grant's army before the arrival of the reinforcements, he was fatally wounded in the leg. The person who assumed command, General P. G. T. Beauregard, was not quick enough to follow up on the initial successes, allowing Buell to save Grant with an additional twenty thousand fresh troops, which arrived on the battlefield early on April 7th. Now at a numerical disadvantage, Beauregard was forced to retreat to Corinth, Mississippi, but had still inflicted considerable casualties to the Union forces, about thirteen thousand men in total, while suffering ten thousand casualties himself.

The Battle of Shiloh was one of the most pivotal early encounters in the Trans-Mississippi campaigns, allowing the Union forces to gain an initial advantage and control large territories in Kentucky and Tennessee. This headway was crucial for the capture of the Mississippi River, which had been one of the original objectives of the Union high command. By capturing and holding the river, the Confederacy would have been split in half, with Texas, Arkansas, and Louisiana being disconnected from the rest of the Southern states in the east. After the relative success at Shiloh and the far less fruitful campaigns in Virginia, the Union's attention shifted to taking control of the Mississippi.

However, the Confederates were not keen on giving up fighting in the west. Beauregard, who was not favored by Jefferson Davis, was eventually replaced by Braxton Bragg as the commander of the Southern forces in the Trans-Mississippi. Acting on Davis's direct orders, Bragg split the army, leaving about twenty thousand men in defense of Mississippi, and ventured out to deal a blow to the Union in Kentucky, starting a campaign known as the Confederate Heartland Offensive. He moved north through Chattanooga with about thirty thousand soldiers and eventually joined up with the Confederate Trans-Mississippi Department under Edmund Kirby Smith, who had additional eighteen thousand men or so at his disposal.

The Confederate campaign was largely successful, gaining significant ground against the disunited Union forces. For instance, with just five thousand men, Smith and the Confederates were able to decisively defeat the Union Army regiments at Richmond, Kentucky, in late August. However, in early October, the Confederate Army came across a larger Union force under

Commander Don Carlos Buell at Perryville, where the two sides engaged in fierce combat for two days. Both sides suffered heavy casualties at about four thousand each, but in the end, Buell and his men stopped Bragg's advance, forcing him to retreat back over the border to Tennessee.

Despite the Union's incapacity to properly punish the numerically inferior enemy, the encounter at Perryville largely determined Kentucky's fate, with the Union gaining firm control over it. In addition to Bragg's retreat from Kentucky, Federal (another name for the Union) forces under William S. Rosecrans were able to overcome the Confederate force that had split off from Bragg at the start of his campaign at Iuka, Mississippi, and later at Corinth, contributing to the weakening of the Confederate positions in the Trans-Mississippi Theater. By late October, the Union forces had assumed a commanding position in the fight for Tennessee, and by the end of the year, in the Battle of Stones River, they were able to gain a close victory against the Confederates. Having suffered about 13,000 casualties to Bragg's 11,700, Commander Rosecrans cemented the Union's control over both Kentucky and Tennessee and eliminated a major point of contention between the two sides.

All in all, the year 1862 proved to be very successful for the Union cause in the Trans-Mississippi since the fight for the border states was largely won thanks to the efforts of commanders Grant, Buell, and Rosecrans. The Confederates had been deprived of resources to use in the war and were forced to retreat from Kentucky and Tennessee farther south to the state of Mississippi, where they put up a final stand at Vicksburg.

Perhaps it is now best to take a look at a very important factor that contributed greatly to the Union's successes in the war, especially in the Trans-Mississippi Theater: the superior Union Navy. With it, the Federals had been able to seize control of the pivotal city of New Orleans in April 1862, something that became a thorn in the side of the Confederate war effort.

Union Naval Supremacy and the Capture of New Orleans

The Union's crucial advantage over the Confederacy did not actually come on the field. It came at sea, as the Northern navy was significantly larger and, therefore, more capable. President Lincoln was also lucky to have a very wise and experienced man as his secretary of the navy, Gideon Welles, a veteran Democrat-turned-Republican. Welles had an ability to correctly understand the most pressing situation and led the Union naval effort throughout the war. Under Welles, the number of men enlisted in the navy increased from nine thousand to about sixty thousand throughout the war, something that greatly contributed to the Northern war effort. With more men and resources, the Union Navy was able to maintain a blockade of the large Confederate coastline, which stretched for about 3,5000 miles—something that had been perceived impossible at the start of the conflict and, in the minds of the Confederates, gave the South a natural advantage over the North.

On the other hand, the Southern navy was not nearly as developed. In fact, compared to the number of ships, guns, and men available to the Northern sea effort, the Confederate Navy was almost laughable at the start of the war. It was thanks to Confederate Secretary of the Navy Stephen Mallory that the Southern coastline was able to hold off the Northern barrages for as long as it did. After the outbreak of the conflict, Mallory commissioned the building of new warships, sent out agents to foreign countries to try and buy ships and sailors to man them, and even paid locals who owned ships to equip them and make them ready for war. For most of the war, the Confederate sea effort was concentrated on disrupting the Union's maritime trade and commerce, with Southern raiders with smaller, faster ships being a thorn in the side of the Union.

An important characteristic of naval warfare during the Civil War is that it coincided with the development of marine military technology, which allowed for new, more resilient, and effective ship designs to emerge throughout the mid-1850s. The new steam engines made naval travel far easier and faster. In addition, the "ironclad" type warship is perhaps one of the most influential inventions of the 19th century, characterized by the use of reinforced iron casemates, which protected the body (the hull) of the ship. They became the most prominent type of warship in the Civil War and were even used in other parts of the world since they dominated the seas and were able to outdo older ships with wooden hulls.

The ironclads were used by both sides in the first naval battle of the Civil War on March 9th, 1862, at Hampton Roads, Virginia, where the Confederates, with the stolen northern ironclad *Virginia*, were able to decimate the wooden Union warships before the arrival of a Union ironclad, *Monitor*. The strength of the ironclads was demonstrated throughout the battle, especially when *Virginia* managed to hold off a whole fleet of wooden warships while suffering insignificant blows.

In addition to coastal warfare on the high seas, a significant part of the Union Army also operated on the Mississippi River, which allowed smaller-scale ironclads to be deployed and utilized as additional support to the army that operated on the field. The wide basin of the Mississippi made transportation by ships easy and efficient, especially considering just how much importance the North assigned to the control of the basin. However, seizing control of the upper course of the river would not be enough to achieve the goal envisioned by the Anaconda Plan. To successfully maintain dominance in the Trans-Mississippi and split off the western Confederacy from the east, the Union high command knew that capturing the city of New Orleans was instrumental.

New Orleans had been one of the largest and fastest-growing cities in the country for decades by the time the war broke out. It was the only city in the South with well over 100,000 citizens and the center of the Southern slave trade. In addition, it was located on the lower end of the Mississippi River and provided a gateway to the Gulf of Mexico and, thus, the Atlantic Ocean. In short, New Orleans was one of the most important cities the Confederates held at the start of the Civil War, holding not only material but also immense symbolic importance, something that had been well realized by the Union high command.

However, getting to New Orleans overland was never considered, despite the fact that the Union Army had seen quite substantial successes in their Trans-Mississippi campaign. The most sensible thing was to task the navy with getting to New Orleans from the sea and establishing temporary control over it before the army could reach it. It was a prime target, an obvious one even, but as it turned out, it was not nearly as well defended as it should have been.

In January 1862, once the war was well underway but before it could really kick off in the Trans-Mississippi, the Union high command put Captain David Farragut in charge of the West Gulf Blockading Squadron, which consisted of four heavy warships, about a dozen-and-a-half smaller gunboats, and twenty mortar boats. Farragut was tasked with taking New Orleans, something which he delivered immaculately. After sailing up to the city's entrance from the south, he came across two fortifications on the Mississippi: Fort Jackson and Fort St. Philip, both of which were firmly built and housed Confederate artillery. They were located on each bank of the river, with an underwater boom—a strong chain designed to keep the vessels from entering narrow points—stretched in between.

After reaching the city on April 16th, Farragut had to fight for a week to break through the forts' defenses, as well as a relatively small fleet defending the city. Confederate Major General Mansfield Lovell, who was in charge of the men in New Orleans, was forced to evacuate the city, knowing that the rest of the defenses were not designed to hold off an amphibious assault and that the Union fleet would soon be reinforced by the army. Thus, he loaded whatever supplies he could gather and fled to Camp Moore and Vicksburg to set up a final Confederate stand in the west. Captain Farragut faced no more resistance, with the forts surrendering on April 28th. He had captured New Orleans, a prized possession of the Confederacy, a city that embodied the spirit of the South, dealing an excruciating blow to the Confederate war effort in the west. On May 1st, Union Army regiments arrived in New Orleans and peacefully occupied the city.

However, the fight for the Trans-Mississippi was not quite over.

Chapter 9 – The War in 1863

After almost two years since the secession of the seven Deep South states, the subsequent formation of the Confederacy, and bloody fighting between the two sides, nobody was still quite sure who had the upper hand in the war. Lincoln's more aggressive approach to the Civil War, caused by his belief that he had every right to protect the unity of the Union, had been somewhat effectively thwarted in Virginia, where the majority of fighting had so far unfolded. The two sides had entered into a stalemate, with neither of them having assumed an advantageous position. In the Trans-Mississippi, however, the Union forces significantly weakened the Confederate opposition, having driven them back from Kentucky and Tennessee. They had captured New Orleans and effectively achieved what had been intended from the very start of the conflict: control over the river and a separation between the eastern and western parts of the Confederacy.

The Vicksburg Campaign

Having taken control of the Lower Mississippi with the capture of New Orleans, one final location the Union needed to cement was its dominance of the city of Vicksburg, which was sometimes referred to as the "Gibraltar of the West" due to the important role of "conductor" it played on the river. It was another prized possession of the Confederates. And with New Orleans gone and the Union troops achieving success in the border states of Missouri and Kentucky, Vicksburg remained the only major connecting point between the western and eastern Confederate states. For this reason, it was heavily fortified and garrisoned, and the defenses were actually able to hold off the Union forces, which had set their eyes on the city in late December 1862.

The early efforts to capture Vicksburg had proven ineffective. Ulysses S. Grant, who was leading the main contingent of the Union forces on land and had maritime support from Admiral Farragut, tried to salvage the situation by attempting to take the city during the Bayou Expeditions in early 1863. However, these expeditions could not gain a significant enough headway to give the North an advantage over the defenders. Frustrated, Grant finally decided to launch one final offensive on Vicksburg, which involved a daring move of crossing the eastern bank of the Mississippi, where the city was located, to its southern flank while being supported by the Union gunboats that would pass the city downstream. The plan was risky because once the gunboats under Admiral David Dixon Porter passed the city and provided artillery support, they would require time to come up the stream to reinforce Grant and his men, leaving them potentially undefended.

In late April 1863, Grant landed south of Vicksburg at Bruinsburg, Mississippi, continuing his move eastward with about thirty thousand men and overcoming a relatively small Confederate resistance at Port Gibson, Raymond, and then Jackson—the capital of Mississippi—all in just the span of two weeks. By mid-May, Grant had seized control of Jackson and cut off the Confederate forces there from joining up with the rest of the army in Vicksburg. Next, he turned west to finally approach the city, achieving even more victories in skirmishes at Champion Hill and Big Black River Bridge until reaching Vicksburg on May 18th. He was finally within striking distance of Vicksburg, but instead of advancing right away with an assault, Grant waited for a couple of weeks, encircling the city to ensure it ran out of supplies. Eventually, he gained more reinforcements, almost doubling his numbers, while Confederate Commander John C. Pemberton inside the city was slowly losing his men due to attrition and desertion.

Vicksburg surrendered on July 4th, 1863, with the Union forces finally taking control of the whole Mississippi River in the coming weeks, giving President Lincoln a sigh of relief and turning the course of the war once again in favor of the Union.

Anti-War Opposition in the North

When the year 1863 rolled around, President Lincoln had nothing to worry about when it came to the Civil War, at least on paper. The war effort had been going strong for about two years, and even if the Union did not see significant successes against the South in Virginia, the situation was drastically different in the west. Domestically, however, even the naked eye could see that things were not as in order as Lincoln would have liked.

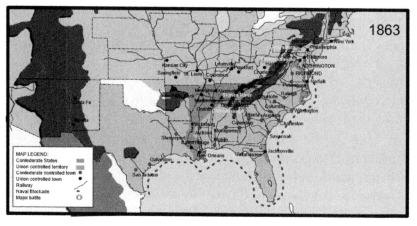

Overview of the American Civil War.
Andrei nacu at the English Wikipedia, CC BY-SA 3.0 <http://creativecommons.org/licenses/by-sa/3.0/>, via Wikimedia Commons, https://commons.wikimedia.org/wiki/File:American_Civil_War_-_Map_Overview_1863.svg

Due to the ambiguous results in Virginia throughout the autumn of 1862, as well as the recent signing of the Emancipation Proclamation, which had angered many anti-abolitionist Democrats, the president was facing a severe political crisis. The public, led by those Democrats who had opposed the war since the very beginning, either wanted decisive results or an end to the whole thing. It was very difficult for Lincoln and his team to effectively communicate to the ordinary Northern citizen that the military campaigns, despite not producing a clear-cut advantage for the Union in the east, were nevertheless successful in the Trans-

Mississippi. It was becoming clear that Lincoln needed to get his house in order if he had any ambition of ending the already dragged-out war and gaining the final victory.

Democrats who were referred to as "Copperheads" by their Republican counterparts led the anti-war opposition. They had been named after a type of poisonous snake. The Copperheads gained much traction in the Union over the autumn. They had gained even more grounds to protest with the passing of the Emancipation Proclamation, believing that the freeing of so many enslaved people would harm the country in the long term. They were mainly comprised of more conservative-leaning groups who believed that Lincoln and the Republicans were violating the Constitution on a daily basis by overexercising their powers. A big number of them were Irish and German immigrants who had come under severe discrimination from the largely Protestant and, in many cases, nativist US public. The Copperheads united around the principle of "The Union as it was, the Constitution as it is," signaling their discontent with the way President Lincoln was handling things but also stating that they condemned the secession of the Confederacy.

In the end, the Copperheads were not able to grow their numbers significantly enough to pose severe problems to Lincoln and his administration, but they did protest almost every decision Congress made throughout the war. In the mid-term elections, although the Republicans had lost some seats, they still managed to gain a convincing majority in both of the legislative bodies of the country and were thus virtually free to pass any new bill they supported. For example, during the war, Congress introduced a new paper currency, which was cheaper to make. The currency slowly started to replace the minted coinage, something the Copperheads thought went against the Constitution. The income tax, among other things, was also protested by the anti-war Democrats.

Chancellorsville and Gettysburg

The decisive action in the east that the anti-war opposition had been asking for would take place in Virginia in the coming months. Lincoln had appointed a new commander to the Army of the Potomac, Fighting Joe Hooker, who, over the winter, had managed to grow the number of his men to about 130,000. The Northern army in the east dwarfed whatever the Confederates had to offer. By comparison, Confederate General Lee only had about sixty-two thousand men at his disposal, and if we take into consideration the array of supply shortages that had plagued his army over the past couple of months, he was at a serious disadvantage.

The stage was set for the continuation of hostilities once the winter cold blew in. After disappointing results at both Antietam and Fredericksburg, Lincoln was hoping to achieve success in the east to calm the protesters back home and show that, in spite of the war dragging on more than anybody had predicted, the Union was still too strong to be overcome by anything the Confederacy could throw at it.

Hooker started his Chancellorsville campaign in the spring of 1863, hoping to capitalize on his numerical advantage and deal a blow to the Confederates at Fredericksburg, the control of which was vital to allow for the safe passage of the Union forces over the Rappahannock River. Hooker hoped to pull off a flanking maneuver, passing the Rappahannock several miles northwest from Fredericksburg, and attack the Confederate forces from the western part of the town. This part of his plan was successful, as the bulk of the Union forces—just short of 100,000 men—crossed the nearby Rapidan River and positioned itself on the Confederate flank. Only a minor portion of the Union Army crossed the river east of Fredericksburg to distract the enemy.

However, to his surprise, Hooker was met with the majority of Lee's troops, which had practically abandoned the town to defend against Hooker's troops that had just crossed the river. Frustrated, Hooker had to order a general retreat westward to the woods of Chancellorsville on May 1ˢᵗ, 1863, while the rest of the Union forces that remained in the eastern part of Fredericksburg were contained by the Confederates. Positioning at Chancellorsville was not ideal because the superior Union artillery was useless in awkward terrain and wilderness, as they blocked its line of sight. As if that was not enough, Lee was quick to follow up with the Union retreat, sending a portion of his forces around Hooker's main line. Commanded by Stonewall Jackson, the Confederate flanking force brilliantly maneuvered its way in the woods of Chancellorsville and burst through the Union's rear on May 2nd, although Commander Jackson was accidentally shot by his own men and died days later.

After hearing of the flanking maneuver's success, Lee ordered the rest of his troops to attack Hooker's front line, converging on all sides and eventually pushing the Union forces back over the Rappahannock River by May 6th. The Union troops that had landed on the eastern side of Fredericksburg were also repelled, marking a decisive Confederate victory at the Battle of Chancellorsville.

The battle had produced a devastating outcome for the Union, with over seventeen thousand casualties to the Confederacy's twelve thousand. This victory boosted the Confederates' morale through the roof, and many people on both sides believed that General Lee was one of the brightest military minds in the history of the United States. His decisive action and clever strategy had yielded successful results for the Southern cause once again, while the North was left empty-handed and disappointed at a pivotal moment in the war. However, as time would show, the victory at Chancellorsville perhaps caused overconfidence in Lee, if not among the whole Confederate Army, prompting the general to embark on a daring campaign to invade the Union for the second time.

It took about a month of preparing for Lee to cross the Rappahannock in early June and invade the Union territories. At that time, the Union forces had retreated farther up north to reinforce and resupply, and the high command was debating what to do next. Historians believe that Lee made this daring decision because he had overestimated the anti-war sentiment in the North. With a quick invasion of the free states, Lee hoped to disrupt whatever plans the Union might have had and encourage the anti-war Copperheads to push for the end of hostilities. However, in reality, the Copperheads represented the opinion of the minority. Most Northerners were inspired and assured by Lincoln and his administration that the Union had a commanding position in the war. They fully believed in the Northern cause. Although they hoped that the war would be over quickly, they were also determined to see the South defeated because they believed the Southern states had unjustly seceded from the Union. Thus, overconfident in the capabilities of his men and banking on several hypothetical outcomes, Lee marched north, still managing to catch the Union high command off-guard.

Heading northwest from Fredericksburg up the Shenandoah Valley, Lee hoped to envelop his forces and surround the bulk of the Union troops on the eastern coast. His movement was mirrored subtly by Hooker and his troops, who were positioned at a distance. They were close enough to engage if necessary but also waited for a bolder advance of the Confederates to assume a more defensive position. The two sides engaged in several skirmishes during Lee's advance throughout early June, first at Brandy Station, then at Winchester, where the Confederates emerged victorious and captured about 4,000 troops while only losing 250 themselves.

Lee continued his march northward, perhaps trying to find a suitable time and place to break through and converge on Washington, but the Union troops were always in a position to intercept. After more small-scale encounters between the two sides, Hooker resigned his position as the commander of the Army of the Potomac after a disagreement with the high command on the matter of additional reinforcements, which he did not receive. In late June, he would be replaced by George Gordon Meade.

By that time, Lee and the Confederates had crossed the border of Pennsylvania. Some of their corps were even stretched all the way northeast up to Harrisburg on the Susquehanna River. The state was swept up in an all-out panic after Lincoln notified the governor of potential Confederate strikes on major towns like Philadelphia and Harrisburg. The president also requested more volunteers to respond to the imminent threat, and defenses were organized in the big cities to hold off a Confederate attack until the main army could reinforce them. Fearing Lee's intentions, the Union high command also ordered a small force of about thirty-two thousand men under Major General John A. Dix to threaten the Confederate capital of Richmond, which had been left relatively undefended, as the vast majority of the Southern troops were with Lee in Pennsylvania.

On June 30th, after about a month of the Union forces chasing Lee's army north of the Rappahannock, the two main armies were dangerously close to each other. A day later, on July 1st, the two sides would engage in the most famous battle of the American Civil War near the town of Gettysburg, Pennsylvania. Gettysburg acted as a gateway to the Confederate forces. If they took control of the town, they would be able to converge on Washington from the north. Thus, the two armies met in the skirmish. Both sides knew of the battle's importance.

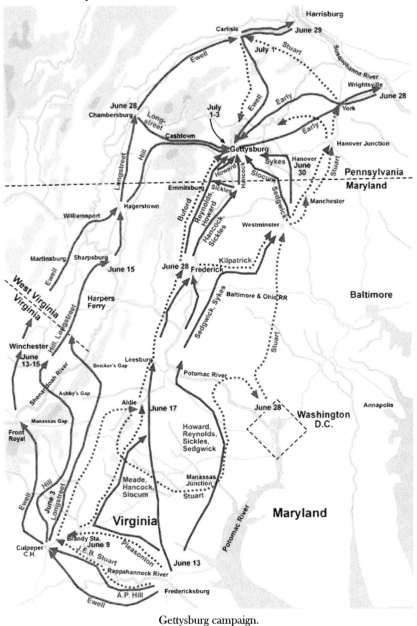

Gettysburg campaign.
https://commons.wikimedia.org/wiki/File:Gettysburg_Campaign_(original).jpg

On the first day of battle, a force of no more than thirty thousand Confederate troops defeated a much smaller Union resistance of about eighteen thousand men commanded by John F. Reynolds. After hours of fighting, the Union forces realized they were being overwhelmed and were forced to retreat, first to the streets of the town and then to the defensive location of Cemetery Hill, just outside of Gettysburg in the south. There, the leftover Union troops met up with the bulk of General Meade's army and awaited the further advance of the Confederates, who had now taken partial control of the town.

On July 2nd, with both armies having been significantly reinforced, Meade organized his ninety-five thousand or so troops in a defensive position, making use of the high terrain, which gave an advantage to the Union artillery. Lee did not try to match the Union front line; instead, he ordered a concentrated attack on Meade's left flank. Led by Confederate General James Longstreet, the Confederates were able to push the Union defensive line farther back but could not fully break through the left flank. Meade was quick to reorganize his defenses to make up for the numerical disadvantage on the left flank and established a new defensive line. The Confederate attack was repulsed.

July 3rd turned out to be decisive for the course of the battle. As Meade's defensive position was proving to be difficult to crack, Lee ordered more than ten thousand men to charge the left center of the Union frontlines. It was an all-out infantry attack, which could likely go either way. Commanded by General George E. Pickett, this move, which began in the afternoon, became known as Pickett's Charge. Although Meade's men were first softened up by artillery, they were shocked that such a large contingent of troops was hurtling right at them with bayonets, especially considering the fact they had the high ground. Despite the hand-to-hand combat going in favor of the Confederates, the Union troops managed to hold their positions. The Confederate soldiers had appeared to have charged to their deaths. They were already missing hundreds by the time they reached the enemy. It was a tragic sight, brothers killing brothers with whatever they could find, even their bare hands.

Eventually, after the massacre had settled, Lee called off the attack and retreated with whatever men were left from the deadly charge. The retreating troops were relentlessly gunned down by Union artillery, and the North finally sighed in relief as the Confederates returned to their positions.

The three days of fighting were equally catastrophic for both sides. The total casualty toll stands anywhere from forty-five thousand to fifty-five thousand. After the Confederate retreat late on July 3rd, Lee decided to give up Gettysburg and retreat to assume a defensive position of his own, confident that Meade would follow up with a counterattack. However, the Union commander, thinking that his forces were exhausted after so much fighting, chose to hold his position—a decision for which he has been criticized by both his contemporaries and historians. Although the Union forces were not in the greatest shape to continue a long-term campaign, a quick follow-up assault on Lee's remaining troops might have sealed the deal in terms of the Confederates' strength to continue the war effort. Still, Meade should be respected for not sending more of his men on an ill-prepared offensive, as it would have only caused the loss of more lives. In the following weeks, smaller Union forces made sure the Confederate Army of Northern Virginia was fully out of Northern territory and had crossed the border back into Virginia.

The Battle of Gettysburg is perhaps the most widely known battle of the Civil War. It remains the bloodiest battle of the war, and although both sides suffered heavy casualties, it is considered a Union victory. General Meade was able to almost flawlessly defend the pivotal town of Gettysburg from falling under the control of the Confederates and forced Lee and his men to abandon their offensive on Union territories. The events that transpired at Gettysburg greatly influenced the development of the war. The Confederates had to suffer a rather disappointing result while having come so close to victory. President Lincoln, on the other hand, could finally present the victory at Gettysburg as not only another valiant effort of the Union soldiers but also as proof to the anti-war opposition that the war was going in the North's favor. Although the war was still far from over, the fatalities suffered by the Confederates, including many veteran soldiers who had greatly developed their skills over the course of the war and different valuable officers who had also demonstrated their various strategic capabilities, would prove to be impossible to overcome.

The Fight for Tennessee

In the summer of 1863, the momentum of the war shifted heavily in favor of the Union. In the east, Meade had been able to drive back the invading Confederate Army of Northern Virginia at Gettysburg. The remarkable efforts of General Grant and Admiral Farragut led to the Union forces taking control of the Mississippi River, further weakening the opposition. Although the war had dragged on for longer than Lincoln had hoped in the beginning, most of the original goals of the Anaconda Plan had been achieved. The Confederacy was split into two down the Mississippi, and the naval blockade was paying off dividends. It was apparent that as time went by, the South was doomed to run out of resources to effectively continue the war effort. However, despite the lack of resources, the strength and resilience of the Confederate soldiers, who were motivated by the Southern cause, would be demonstrated once again.

After the defeat of the Confederates at Gettysburg and Grant's successful Vicksburg campaign, the fighting would slowly shift eastward from the Mississippi to the central Confederate territories. Thanks to the efforts of Commander Rosecrans, the Union had already established control over Kentucky and most of Tennessee, with the next main objective being the town of Chattanooga, located on the Tennessee River in the southern part of the state. Capturing Chattanooga would eliminate another major center of the South. It was also a crucial railway connector. It was a natural target for the North, something that had been realized by the Confederate high command, which had tasked General Bragg with the defense of the territory with more than forty thousand soldiers. After General Lee's unsuccessful offensive, a portion of the Confederate Army of Northern Virginia was transported to Chattanooga to reinforce Bragg and make sure that Rosecrans and the Federals would not break through. Out of the three main Union armies, Rosecrans had the most natural path to the city. Having encountered Bragg before at Stone River, he was tasked with capturing the important Tennessean town.

Coming fresh off his success at the Tullahoma campaign, Rosecrans continued to chase down the Confederate troops and drive them back to the other side of the river. However, Bragg, having just been reinforced by the contingents from Lee's army, decided to adopt an active approach and tried to cut off Rosecrans's men. Thus, after a whole month of being chased throughout central and southern Tennessee, Bragg confronted the Union Army southeast of Chattanooga in mid-September at a location called Chickamauga Creek. In a two-day battle, thanks to a miscommunication error on the side of the Union and to the battle being one of the rare instances where the Confederates were not actually heavily outnumbered, Bragg was able to rout Rosecrans and force him to retreat to Chattanooga, where the Confederate commander had the Northern army almost entirely encircled. It was one of the few victories the South gained in the western campaign, but it still inflicted serious casualties on both sides: more than eighteen thousand on the side of the Confederacy and about seventeen thousand on the side of the Union.

Rosecrans found himself now trapped in Chattanooga, besieged by Bragg, who, despite his previous victory, did not have enough resources to force a fight with the Union forces in the city. During the next few weeks, the latter tried to cut off the Union's supply lines in Chattanooga, perhaps hoping that either he would get reinforced or that Rosecrans would give up. However, it was all in vain. After hearing of Rosecrans's defeat at Chickamauga Creek and realizing the possible consequences that could follow the army's surrender, Lincoln quickly tasked the other commanders with relieving the entrapped Rosecrans. First, an additional twenty thousand men, under the command of Major General "Fighting Joe" Hooker of the Army of the Potomac, were immediately sent by rail to reinforce Commander Rosecrans. In addition, Ulysses S. Grant, who was also appointed as the commander of the newly established Union Military Division of the Mississippi, which incorporated all the armies in the western theater, headed east from Vicksburg to Chattanooga in late September. Arriving in the Tennessean city on October 22nd, Grant was determined to keep the city and not give it up under any circumstances, even if it meant vicious fighting.

With the arrival of reinforcements, the balance of power swung in favor of the Union. Grant, who had assumed command of the united force, now outnumbered Bragg's Confederate Army by about ten thousand. Although there were still supply problems, Grant launched an offensive on the besieging Confederates in late November and was able to defeat them at the battles of Orchard Knob and Lookout Mountain. By November 25th, the Union forces were able to capture the strategically important Missionary Ridge near Chattanooga, gaining the high ground and forcing Bragg to issue a full-on retreat. The Confederates retreated to Chickamauga, where they utilized the rail to flee to Georgia. The fight for Tennessee was over, with the Union suffering about 5,800 casualties to the Confederacy's 6,600.

After gaining firm control of Chattanooga, the Union stripped the Confederacy from a lot of its core territories. The deadlock still existed in the east, with the front lines having changed inconsequentially after the start of the war. But thanks to the efforts of General Grant and the rest of the forces who fought in the west, the North now controlled all of the Mississippi Basin, the crucial border states of Missouri and Kentucky, and Confederate territories east of the Mississippi, including the states of Mississippi, a large part of Louisiana and Arkansas, and all of Tennessee. Only the modern southeastern states were still under the Confederates' control, but there, too, existed a myriad of problems that were linked with the war effort.

Davis and the Southern government diverted the majority of the country's resources, everything from food to clothes to the army, leaving the Southern population upset and on the verge of starvation. The South was also quickly running out of men, and new conscription laws, which first required all capable men aged eighteen to thirty-five to enlist, were later extended to all men aged between seventeen and fifty. This caused the wealthier Southerners, who had no intention of fighting, to hire replacements who could serve instead of them, causing even more anti-war sentiment among the commoners. They often called the conflict "a war of the rich, but the fight of the poor."

With the Southern economy collapsing, its population greatly upset, and the Union pressing forward at a steady pace, it was only a matter of time until the North gained a decisive advantage and emerged victorious from the Civil War, a detail that was realized by both sides by the end of 1863.

Chapter 10 – The Final Campaigns

The year 1863 had proven to be the most decisive in the war, with the Union assuming a clear advantage over the Confederacy by achieving important victories on all fronts. In the east, General Meade and the Army of the Potomac were able to successfully drive the Confederate offensive back at Gettysburg, dealing a catastrophic blow to the Southern war effort and punishing Confederate General Lee for his overconfidence and overzealousness to invade the Northern territories. In the west, through the efforts of Ulysses S. Grant, the Union had gained a significant advantage and achieved the original intended goal of the war by splitting the South into two along the Mississippi River and making it more difficult for it to continue the war. Then, despite initial setbacks at Tennessee and Mississippi, the Union forces managed to overcome the Confederate defenses and gain control of some of the key Southern states, giving them direct access to the Confederate heartland. Finally, the superiority of the Northern fleet at sea and the effective naval blockade it had maintained for much of the war had reduced the Southern economy to dust and further pressured President Jefferson Davis to come up with an effective response.

The Overland Campaign

After Chattanooga, no major campaigns were immediately started by both sides, as they decided to wait out the winter in their respective camps and replenish their losses. President Lincoln had noticed Grant's successes and liked him for his resilient personality and outlook on the war. So, in early 1864, Lincoln appointed Grant as the new general in chief, replacing Halleck. The new general in chief visited the capital in the spring of 1864 to discuss his strategy and the intended objectives for the Union forces. Having left the command of his forces in the west to William Tecumseh Sherman, Grant did not assume direct control of the Army of the Potomac himself, leaving Meade in his position.

From the very beginning, Lincoln and his Cabinet trusted Grant to deliver, and Grant would be actively involved for the remainder of the war in all of the military developments, which earned him great popularity among his contemporaries. Eventually, he would become the eighteenth president of the United States.

Realizing the Union's advantageous position, Lincoln and Grant hoped to deal fatal blows to the South from all sides. The Army of the Potomac would start an offensive against the main Confederate force under Lee and try to take Richmond. Simultaneously, the newly appointed commander of the western armies, Major General Sherman, would lead his men to Georgia with the objective of capturing Atlanta. Union Commander Franz Sigel was tasked with attacking the crucial fields in the Shenandoah Valley. Nathaniel Banks would split off from Sherman to take control of Alabama. And finally, the Union forces under George Crook were tasked with taking control of the Confederate supply lines in West Virginia. Together, these armies should overwhelm anything the South could provide. It was the first instance in the war that the Union forces would conduct a coordinated offensive on all fronts. Often referred to as the "Overland Campaign," it marked the successful culmination of the Union war effort.

The Overland Campaign started in early May, with Grant leading the Army of the Potomac over the Rappahannock River in Virginia, approaching Wilderness Tavern west of Chancellorsville. Lee noticed Grant's movements and was quick to react, confronting the Union Army on May 5th. The Battle of the Wilderness lasted for two straight days. The Confederates were able to use the surprise factor in their favor and inflicted about 18,000 casualties to Grant's 110,000-strong force (the Confederates only had about 60,000 men with them). This maneuver forced Grant to assume a defensive position, and he ordered a retreat, despite the fact that the South did not gain a convincing victory.

The Union general decided to pull away from the battle and lick his wounds while continuing his march southeast. He would be met with Confederate forces at Spotsylvania Court House. The two sides engaged fiercely on May 7th with their cavalry regiments, with both trying to gain a more advantageous position for the ensuing battle. In the following days, Lee unsuccessfully tried to outflank Grant's front line, although it did seem like the Confederates were gaining the upper hand despite their inferior numbers. By May 12th, a Confederate offensive made a slight gap in the Union defenses, but General Grant was quick to focus his reinforcements on containing the breakthrough while maneuvering the remainder of his army to create a new front line on the eastern side of the battlefield.

When the fighting ended on May 19th, neither side had gained anything valuable. Although Grant suffered another eighteen thousand or so casualties in the battle, he had many more men at his disposal to continue his campaign. The Confederates, who had lost no more than twenty thousand men since the start of Grant's offensive, did not press forward, fearing that further losses would be detrimental in the long term.

After the events at Spotsylvania, Grant decided to continue his advance southeast, racing Lee's men to the Confederate capital of Richmond. The two forces mirrored each other's movements and slowly made their way to Richmond, engaging multiple times over the next few weeks. The Confederates were able to utilize the Virginia railroads, which were not accessible to the Union, to match Grant's movements and deny them a closer approach to Richmond a couple of times, like at North Anna and Totopotomoy Creek. Lee would always be there first, forcing Grant to fight in unfavorable conditions. In early June, as the fighting had shifted farther south and was dangerously close to the capital, Grant crossed the Pamunkey River and confronted the Confederates at Cold Harbor, which lay just northeast of Richmond

By that point, Grant had lost about fifty thousand men during his campaign, but he had also taken the fight to Lee and posed a real threat to Richmond. The Confederates at Cold Harbor assumed favorable defensive positions, having entrenched themselves and set up artillery. For two days, several separate Union attacks were repelled by the defenders, who were putting up a good fight despite being outnumbered. Then, on June 3rd, Grant ordered a massive frontal assault on the Confederates—a move that has been deemed borderline suicidal by historians. Engaging with his 2nd, 6th, and 18th Corps early in the morning fog, the Union forces were forced to charge through difficult terrain. They became stuck in the mud and swamps, making them an easy target for the entrenched Confederates. Up to twelve thousand Union men died in the battle, which was finally recalled by Grant once he realized the South was not about to break as he had hoped.

After being forced to leave the battlefield without the results he had hoped for but having softened up the Confederate forces, Grant decided to continue his movement southward. He aimed to reach the town of Petersburg, Virginia, on the Appomattox River. Still, Lee was adamant about confronting Grant at every possible opportunity that presented itself. His troops, exhausted from the constant marching and fighting, still continued to defensively mirror the Union forces and stop them from gaining access to crucial locations, including Petersburg, which they defended fiercely. The Confederates held off the Union attacks from June 9th to June 18th at the outskirts of the town, not allowing them to take control of Petersburg, which would cut off a crucial supply line to Richmond and open up the southern capital for a Union offensive.

With more than eight thousand Union men lost in the encounters at Petersburg and fearing that further losses would demoralize his troops, who had seen enough action over the course of May and June, Grant decided to settle for a long and tiresome siege of Petersburg in late June. By then, he had realized he could not gain the upper hand on Lee, as his attempts to outflank the Confederates had proven ineffective. Constructing a long trench line while not fully surrounding Petersburg, Grant besieged the Army of the Potomac for nine months, beginning in late June 1864. The Overland Campaign had not yielded the results he had initially hoped for, perhaps because the Confederates realized that giving up ground near Richmond would be fatal for them. Still, despite Grant's relatively unsuccessful effort to capture Richmond, he was counting on the other armies operating in the west to pressure the Confederate defenders to give up.

Into the Confederate Heartland

As Grant attempted to break through Lee's forces and get to Richmond, Commander Sherman, now in charge of the western armies, was closing in on Atlanta. Fielding more than 110,000 men, Sherman's forces outnumbered whatever resistance the Confederacy could offer in this theater. Commander Johnston was in charge of the Confederate Army in the west, but he only commanded about half the men available to Sherman, giving the North a clear advantage once again.

The campaign to capture Atlanta greatly resembled Grant's efforts. The Union Army marched south from Chattanooga while being matched by the Confederates at every step of the way. After heading south from Dalton, Georgia, light skirmishes broke out between contingents of the two armies throughout early May at Resaca and Adairsville. Johnston knew he had the numerical disadvantage and did not opt for a full-on large-scale fight. Sherman, just like Grant, was trying to outflank the defenders and often sent large portions of his forces on daring maneuvers, but the gradual Confederate retreat made it impossible to catch the Southerners and force them into a head-to-head battle.

This constant cat-and-mouse game arguably favored neither side, but Sherman was still inching forward. The situation was so frustrating that in late June, after countless smaller raids by the Confederate cavalry, Sherman ordered a massive full-frontal assault at Kennesaw Mountain. His impatience proved to be deadly for the Union, as thousands fell victim to the Confederate soldiers' guns. The Confederates had assumed a defensive position up a slope and largely free-fired for most of the battle. Sherman called off the attack eventually, and the Confederates decided to retreat back to Atlanta to organize a final defense. Still, despite these setbacks, the Union forces moved forward at a slow and steady pace.

After the battle at Kennesaw Mountain, Commander Sherman was in reach of Atlanta and had the manpower to lay siege to the city. Confederate Commander Johnston realized the severity of the situation and contacted Jefferson Davis to tell him that fighting for Atlanta would be a lost cause since the Union was just too strong to defeat fully. The answer from Davis was just what one might expect; Johnston was relieved from his command and replaced by John B. Hood, a veteran of the war who had fought at Gettysburg and Chickamauga. One of his legs had been amputated, and his arm was permanently damaged after being shot. Hood, unlike Johnston, was not about to give up without a last stand and decided to sally out from the city and engage Sherman's army on a couple of different occasions.

The newly appointed Confederate commander was unable to stop the Union's advance, despite putting up a fierce fight in each of the battles, first at Peachtree Creek, then at Atlanta, then Ezra Church, and, finally, after being driven back from the outskirts of the city, at Jonesboro. Sherman managed to take control of Atlanta by late August, and the Confederates were forced to abandon the city on September 1ˢᵗ, calling for an evacuation. After taking Atlanta, Sherman decided to wait for a little bit to give his men time to rest and fix the supply issues he had been facing throughout his march. He split off a number of his troops and sent them to Nashville to repel a Confederate attack. Then, Sherman enquired about the situation in the other theaters of war. Around a month and a half later, he embarked on what has been deemed his "March to the Sea."

On November 15ᵗʰ, Sherman took his forces from Atlanta to the east with one goal in mind: to reach the Atlantic coast of Georgia and lay waste to every possible Southern resource on his way. During his thirty-seven-day journey from Atlanta to the town of Savannah, Sherman and about sixty-two thousand Union soldiers covered nearly three hundred miles and destroyed important industrial and agrarian holdings in Georgia. The Union soldiers went after nearly everything, from farms to railroads, and made sure that one of the most pivotal states of the Confederacy had nothing left to contribute to the Southern war effort. Their actions also had a grave psychological impact on the Southern population, which witnessed the relentless destruction of resources. Although Sherman had instructed his soldiers not to touch private property unless provoked, many of them ran rampant with the possibility of demonstrating their power to ordinary Southern citizens. Hundreds of slaves, seeing that the Union Army was close, ran off from their masters and joined the forces.

Sherman's March to the Sea
https://commons.wikimedia.org/wiki/File:F.O.C._Darley_and_Alexander_Hay_Ritchie_-_Sherman%27s_March_to_the_Sea.jpg

The March to the Sea is often classified as an instance of "total war"—an approach to war that favors the idea that one should do everything in their power to gain an advantage over the enemy. Sherman, as well as Grant, are thought to have been firm believers in total war. Although no civilians were reportedly killed during Sherman's brutal march, Georgia suffered irreparable damage to its economy, and Georgians personally hated Sherman for what he had done to the state. The March to the Sea remains one of the most dreadful events of the American Civil War and is a great example of the extent the two sides were willing to go to gain an advantage.

The Fall of Virginia

Having rampaged through Georgia before reaching the Atlantic coastline, Sherman was in position to transfer his troops north and close in on Virginia from the south, while Grant and the Army of the Potomac simultaneously attacked from the north. This would mark the Union's final large-scale military campaign in the war and would conclude the original plan that had been agreed upon by Grant, Lincoln, and the rest of the Union high command during Grant's visit to Washington. By the end of 1865, the Union controlled not only the disputed border states but also large parts of Tennessee, Louisiana, Mississippi, Arkansas, and Georgia. The Confederacy's days were numbered. Their territories were divided, and their armies were scattered in different areas and lacked resources.

Like the March to the Sea, Sherman and his sixty thousand or so men destroyed everything of military value on their way through the Carolinas. Historians argue that this measure was not nearly as necessary as it was in Georgia and that it was only taken to have a further psychological effect on the Southern forces. Many Northerners, including the ones in Sherman's army, believed that South Carolina was responsible for the start of the conflict since it had been the first state to secede from the Union and encouraged the others to join. Thus, when Sherman started to move toward Columbus, South Carolina, in early January 1865, he ordered his men to bring destruction upon the state.

The Confederates had significantly fewer men. The Confederate Army of the Tennessee, battered from constant unsuccessful engagements, numbered fewer than ten thousand men by the spring of 1865 and could not put up a fight against Sherman and his mighty Union force. Several skirmishes broke out between the opposing forces during the late winter, such as the one at the Rivers' Bridge in early February, but it was clear from the beginning that the Federals were too strong to be stopped. On February 17th, Columbus surrendered to Sherman, and the city of Charleston was evacuated by the Southerners. In Columbus, hundreds of slaves and captured Union soldiers were freed, and Sherman's men lavishly celebrated their triumph, something that resulted in a fire that spread throughout the center of the city before it was contained, destroying much of Columbus in the process. While some argue that the fire was accidental, others claim that it was an act of vengeance from the Union troops—an act to demonstrate the North's superiority over the South.

Sherman pushed northward to North Carolina, where he fought a series of battles against the Confederate forces throughout March. After these initial encounters, the town of Fayetteville was captured on March 11th. After the Battle of Bentonville about ten days later, Sherman had eliminated all Confederate resistance in the area, pushing the remnants of the Southern army to Virginia. The Union armies were now at the southern doorstep of Virginia.

Meanwhile, in Virginia, the Union siege of Petersburg was still underway. The Northern forces had established a very long front line, from the southern part of Petersburg all the way to Richmond, and outnumbered the enemy two to one. They wanted to stretch the Confederate forces thin. The siege, which lasted for nine months, proved to be very difficult for General Lee and his fifty thousand or so men. The Union forces had virtually cut off all important railroad access points to Richmond and Petersburg, and Sherman's victories in the south meant that it was only a matter of time before Virginia would run out of supplies and fall to the North. The Confederates could not gain any significant advantage in the skirmishes that broke out during the nine-month period along the front lines. Instead, Grant was slowly waiting out Lee. Grant did not want to commit a lot of men to storm the cities, knowing that it would cost the lives of thousands.

In a desperate attempt to drive the Union forces back, Lee gathered up the majority of his men and ordered them to engage in a concentrated attack on one of the defensive Union locations at Fort Stedman. Lee realized that inaction would only be signing his death warrant, especially with the Union forces under Philip Sheridan slowly approaching to reinforce the siege from the south. Thus, in late March, he trusted the command of around ten thousand men to Major General John B. Gordon and tasked him to try and break through the Union defenses at Fort Stedman, south of Petersburg, which would, in theory, give the Confederate forces a headway to organize more cohesive offensives and maybe even take back control of the railroads.

However, the assault proved to be inconsequential for the Southern cause, as the Confederates suffered about four thousand casualties while not achieving anything of significance. On March 25th, as fighting at Fort Stedman had ceased, it became clear to Lee that he stood no chance. On April 1ˢᵗ, the Union forces followed up their success at Fort Stedman with a complete victory at the Battle of Five Forks. The Union soldiers were ready to converge on Petersburg.

On April 2ⁿᵈ, Lee ordered a general retreat from both Petersburg and Richmond, evacuating the cities and fleeing southwest along the Appomattox River, although this was in vain. Grant chased the remnants of the Confederate forces for about ninety miles, finally catching up to them at Amelia Court House and cutting off their only path to flee.

On April 9ᵗʰ, in what became one of the most important events in American history, Confederate General Lee was forced to meet with the Union high command at Appomattox Court House, where he surrendered the Army of Northern Virginia to Grant. A preliminary ceasefire between the two sides was signed, marking the beginning of the end for the Confederacy.

Chapter 11 – Aftermath

With Lee's surrender at Appomattox Court House on April 9th, 1865, the Confederacy's days were numbered. Technically, the war was not officially over, as the remnants of the Confederate Army were still at large in several different locations.

The War Ends

Although Lee surrendered the Army of Northern Virginia to Grant on April 9th, the fighting between the Confederates and the Federals did not cease right away. A number of smaller Southern forces were still scattered around the country and were hoping to put up a final stand against the Union. Still, much of the fighting after April was pointless and yielded no results whatsoever for the Confederacy.

The word of Lee's surrender spread throughout the United States, reaching the ear of Major General Johnston, who was in charge of the Army of the Tennessee—the second-largest Confederate force after Lee's. Following Lee's surrender, Union cavalry units from General Sherman's army quickly reached Johnston and offered him the chance to surrender, additionally proposing peace terms to take to President Davis. Davis and his Cabinet refused the proposed agreement because they thought it was too humiliating for the South and ordered Johnston to put up a last stand—an order that was smartly refused by Johnston, who chose to save his men and surrendered to Sherman in late April.

Lee's surrender

By signing the agreement, all the troops in the Confederate states east of the Mississippi were given up, and the fighting largely ceased in this part of the country. The Confederate forces under Lieutenant General Richard Taylor in Alabama—about ten thousand men—surrendered on May 4th. This was followed by the capture of President Davis in Georgia, whose government had crumbled in the face of the Union victory and had lost all legitimacy by April. Davis had been on the run since the evacuation of Richmond in early April. Since then, he had traveled south with the remnants of his government, trying to evade the Northern forces, but he eventually realized that his fate had been sealed. On May 9th, a month after Lee's surrender at Appomattox Court House, Davis and his men were captured by the Union forces, who, by that time, suspected that he had instigated the assassination of President Lincoln a month before. He was taken to Fort Monroe in Virginia, where he spent the next two years.

Despite these events, the fighting had not ceased west of the Mississippi, where Confederate Lieutenant General Kirby Smith was in control of the South's final army. However, since Lee's surrender, his army had been slowly disintegrating. Three days after the capture of Jefferson Davis, the final land battle between the Union and the Confederacy unfolded in Texas, where about 600

Union troops under Colonel Theodore H. Barrett engaged with about 350 Southerners under the command of Colonel. John Ford. Although the fighting in Texas had stopped by then, the relatively inexperienced Barrett ordered an assault on the Confederate force and suffered a close defeat at the Battle of Palmito Ranch. As one can imagine, this engagement was inconsequential. Confederate Lieutenant General Smith surrendered his force on May 26th.

Interestingly, the last Confederate surrender would take place in modern-day Oklahoma, which had been declared "Indian Territory" during the Civil War. About a month after Smith's surrender, Confederate Brigadier General Stand Watie—the first Native American to serve as a commander in the Civil War—finally gave up his forces, which largely consisted of Native American fighters, at Fort Towson.

The American Civil War was finally over.

A New Age

While the last of the Confederate forces were surrendering throughout the country, important events were transpiring in the North.

President Lincoln's Emancipation Proclamation, which had gone into effect on January 1st, 1863, had proven extremely effective. As we have already discussed, thousands of slaves left their masters and fled northward, even joining the Union Army in the fight for their freedom. This had catastrophic effects on the Confederacy's economic and social life and contributed to the North's victory.

Since 1863, Lincoln had spoken on a number of occasions about the gradual abolishment of slavery as a whole, something that sparked debate among the Democrats and the Republicans. Slavery was still in full effect in the four border states since Lincoln knew that upsetting these slave-owning states with emancipation would make them hostile toward the Union. When Lincoln had first run for president, his party platform clearly stated that the Republicans opposed the expansion of slavery to the newly acquired territories of the US, not its complete abolishment. This had been misunderstood by the slave-owning South, which blamed Lincoln for deliberately trying to sabotage their lives and enforce the tyranny of the North. For a similar reason, many Northern Democrats, who had historically opposed the complete abolishment of slavery, feared the material disadvantages it would bring to millions of people. Some outright believed that God had made blacks purposefully inferior to whites. Regardless, the abolishment of slavery moved up on the Republican agenda, and in-party consultations had already started to discuss the matter.

In late 1863, Representative James Mitchell Ashley of Ohio proposed a new constitutional amendment that would end slavery in the United States. This proposal saw overwhelming support from the party. In February 1864, led by the efforts of radical abolitionist Republicans Charles Sumner of Massachusetts and Thaddeus Stevens of Pennsylvania, an amendment proposing the permanent abolishment of slavery was submitted to the Senate. Two months later, in April 1864, the Senate easily passed the new amendment by a vote of thirty-eight to six, gaining the required two-thirds majority. The amendment was now up for the House of Representatives to vote on, which needed three-fourths of all votes.

In June, a new problem presented itself to Lincoln and the Republicans—the House rejected the new amendment, with ninety-three votes in favor and sixty-five against. Thirteen additional votes were needed to pass the amendment, and with the Democrats overwhelmingly opposing it and the new presidential elections just around the corner, it seemed as if the matter would be forever stalled.

What followed next was months of clever political maneuvering by Lincoln and his colleagues to assure they would gain enough support for the amendment in the House. The first major event was Lincoln's reelection in the autumn of 1864. In his platform, he stated that he supported abolition, something that guaranteed his victory. After his reelection and as the Union was gaining a demonstrable advantage in the war, Lincoln envisioned the passing of the new constitutional amendment as an assurance that his fight against slavery would not be in vain. Perhaps the president feared that the Emancipation Proclamation, which he had passed during wartime, would be deemed unjust or get reversed after the end of the war.

Thus, determined to have the proposed abolishment added to the Constitution, Lincoln devised a plan to gain as much support from Congress as he could, knowing that, come spring of 1865, many of the existing congressmen would be gone. Many were "lame ducks," meaning their replacements had already been elected. Lincoln identified these lame ducks, mostly Democrats, and hoped to convince them to vote for the amendment before they left office.

The president tasked Secretary of State Seward with this job, and the latter delivered. In the span of three months, he approached the outgoing Democrats and offered them assurances in the form of government jobs after their leave of office in return for their votes. By then, a few Democrats had already publicly stated they were in favor of the amendment, something that facilitated the process a bit for Seward. Still, Seward, acting on Lincoln's direct orders, outright bribed a handful of Democrats and did everything in his power to get them to vote for the amendment. Although President Lincoln's involvement in the process has never been truly identified, Senator Stevens, the author of the amendment, stated, "The greatest measure of the nineteenth century was passed by corruption aided and abetted by the purest man in America."

In a hurry to pass the amendment before the end of the war, Lincoln pushed the House to vote on it on a number of occasions. Finally, on January 31ˢᵗ, 1865, the House convened to vote on the matter. The session had an unusually large audience, mostly people of color who had been allowed to attend the sessions after emancipation. In a close vote, the Republicans managed to get 119 votes from the representatives—just two more than what they needed to achieve a two-thirds majority. Along with all of the Republicans, fourteen Democrats voted in favor, including those convinced by Seward. Freedom had triumphed.

The new Thirteenth Amendment read: "Neither slavery nor involuntary servitude, except as a punishment for crime whereof the party shall have been duly convicted, shall exist within the United States, or any place subject to their jurisdiction." It was a historic day for the United States and the democratic world. The attendees rejoiced in Congress, with some being reduced to tears, and city-wide celebrations started in Washington. Slavery had finally been abolished.

The Assassination of President Lincoln and the Reconstruction

Chronologically, the Thirteenth Amendment was followed by the victorious Union campaigns in Georgia, the Carolinas, and Virginia. By early April, it was clear the war would be over soon, and everyone in the North breathed a sigh of relief. On April 9th, Lee surrendered the largest Confederate force to Grant, starting a chain reaction that eventually led to the complete defeat of the Confederacy. However, President Lincoln, the man who had engineered both the military victory in the Civil War and perhaps the greatest achievement of American politics in the 19th century, did not live long enough to see the end of the conflict.

On April 14th, just five days after Lee's surrender, President Lincoln was shot at Ford's Theater in Washington, DC. His assassin, a well-known actor named John Wilkes Booth, shot the president in the head while the latter was attending the play *Our American Cousin*. The assassination was part of a larger underground conspiracy plan to undermine the North in the war and gain public support for the Southern cause. Lincoln died the next morning in the Peterson House opposite the theater, but the plan to murder the rest of the leaders in the Union failed, with Secretary of State Seward being only wounded and Vice President Andrew Johnson's assassin never reaching his target.

The assassination of Abraham Lincoln.
https://commons.wikimedia.org/wiki/File:Lincoln_assassination_slide_c1900_-_Restoration.jpg

John Wilkes Booth evaded the authorities for twelve days until he was finally found and shot in Virginia, just south of the Rappahannock River. The rest of the conspirators, who had devised an elaborate plan to extend the Confederacy's fight in the war, were subsequently captured and hanged.

As America mourned Lincoln's death, Vice President Andrew Johnson was sworn in as president, just hours after Lincoln had passed away. As the seventeenth president of the United States, Johnson had arguably just as difficult a task to accomplish as Lincoln: to lead the country through the period immediately after the war, something that, in the face of Lincoln's untimely death, seemed even harder.

The period of recovery after the war would come to be known as the Reconstruction. In fact, the Union government had started thinking about the Reconstruction in 1863 after Lincoln passed the Emancipation Proclamation. Lincoln and his administration proposed the so-called "Ten Percent Plan," which proposed the election of new governments in seceded states if one-tenth of their population swore loyalty to the federal government. However, in 1863, the plan was not that developed, and it certainly did not address many of the problems that would arise once the conflict effectively came to an end. Mainly, there was the question of what exactly to do with all the freed slaves after emancipation had been applied to all of the territories. With no more slavery in the country, were the freed slaves allowed to vote? Did they have the same rights?

Immediately after Johnson became president, he started the initial stage of the Reconstruction, often referred to as the Presidential Reconstruction, which lasted for about two years. He pardoned most of the seceded Southerners except those who had held positions of power in the Confederate government and restored their pre-war properties to them, except for their former slaves, of course. Then, he laid out the plan for the organization of local governments in the former seceded states. Johnson required that they accept the abolition of slavery and reject the secession. In return, he repealed their debt and gave them relative freedom in forming their new state legislatures.

However, despite these measures and the fact that a lot of the Southern population were former slaves, the anti-black sentiment had persevered in the South. The states enacted the so-called "Black Codes," which were laws that forced the newly freed slaves to sign labor contracts with whites. The Black Codes essentially replaced traditional slavery in the Southern states, limiting the social and economic options of the emancipated population and requiring them to continue living in conditions that were similar to the ones they had during slavery.

The new Southern laws sparked a series of protests, including in Congress, where Radical Republicans Stevens and Sumner—two of the authors of the Thirteenth Amendment—proposed that the newly created local Southern governments be dismantled and new ones that respected the equality of all citizens and not treat the freed African Americans as slaves be established. Despite the soundness of their argument and the fact that most African Americans in the South were struggling under the Black Codes, President Johnson opposed the idea, perhaps due to his personal opinions on the matter of race and beliefs on states' rights.

Over time, especially after the congressional elections of 1866, the Northern voters showed overwhelming support for the Radicals Republicans' proposals. The Reconstruction entered a new period, often called the Congressional Reconstruction. After 1867, the Radical Republicans led the effort to reorganize the Southern states and end the injustice of inequality that had existed there for ages. Congress passed the Fourteenth Amendment a year later, a crucial piece of legislation that granted citizenship to almost everyone born in the United States (barring women and Native Americans), guaranteeing that people of color were just as much American as the whites. In the following years, as the formerly seceded states were gradually readmitted to the Union and had all of their rights reinstated, the Reconstruction proved more beneficial than in its first two years, making sure that the Civil War was truly over.

In the long run, the Northern Republicans were able to lead the Reconstruction efforts and ensured that the gap between the North and the South was reduced significantly in all aspects, especially in regard to education. The federal government sponsored the construction of free public schools and universities and also helped the South rebuild its economy around agriculture, which proved to be possible to maintain even though there were no more slaves to work the fields. New manufacturing factories and railroads popped up all over the former Confederate territory with the aim of modernizing all of America as quickly as possible. In addition, the South soon became actively involved in the country's politics, something that had been one of the federal government's priorities to make sure that the Southerners felt like they were not marginalized. The Fifteenth Amendment granted African Americans the right to vote, a natural progression after emancipation and citizenship. Soon, more and more African Americans became involved in politics, and some were even elected to Congress.

Eventually, the Democrats gained control back in the South, passing the infamous Jim Crow laws, which were also passed in the North. These laws made life more difficult for African Americans. For instance, poll taxes and literacy tests discouraged African

Americans from voting. This meant African Americans could not serve on juries or run for office, which practically guaranteed that things would not change any time soon.

In the end, the Reconstruction, although flawed in some regards, was a very influential period of American history, lasting up until the year 1877 when Congress officially pulled the remainder of its troops from the Southern territories. It achieved its main purpose of ending the secessionist sentiment in the Southern states and making them feel as if they were part of the same nation as the North. On the other hand, the emancipated African Americans, although formally declared equal to the white citizens, continued to be discriminated against for nearly one hundred more years. It would not be until the civil rights movement of the 1960s that the American public finally addressed the disenfranchisement that had persevered in the country for much longer than it should have.

Conclusion

The American Civil War remains one of the most influential events of the 19th century. It stands out as one of the most iconic due to the significant part it played in contributing to form a more democratic, free world. No one really knows what would have happened if the Confederacy had emerged victorious in the conflict. Although historians debate the possibility of a Southern victory, it has to be said that the South put up a much better fight than what everyone expected at the beginning of the war. The "Southern cause," a concept that might have seemed too abstract for outsiders, was deemed as something worth fighting for by each Confederate, who, despite being outnumbered at almost every instance, believed they were not on the wrong side of history.

The Civil War is perhaps the best example of what can happen in a country that is divided due to different interpretations of the country's foundations. In the early 19th century, more and more Americans recognized that a society built on the practice of slavery could not fully flourish and act as a beacon of democracy in the world. The divide between the North and the South thus became steeper and steeper. The two sides developed differently for decades, almost to the point that each was its own separate country by the time the war came about. This level of polarization proved to be fatal for the United States, a country that learned the hard way of what can follow if one constantly avoids a problem. For decades, US politicians tried to deal with slavery, but they never succeeded in finding a long-term solution.

Still, the modern United States was forged from these mistakes, and many significant improvements were the byproduct of the bloody war that cost the lives of more than one million Americans, including innocent citizens. The Thirteenth, Fourteenth, and Fifteenth Amendments were the first steps toward an America that truly guaranteed liberty and equality of all peoples against the law, regardless of their race. Abraham Lincoln, the man who led the Union through one of the toughest times in American history, is rightfully credited for his achievements, and it is not hard to see why he is adored by almost everyone. Who knows how he would have led the country after the war? What further improvements would he have been the author of if it weren't for his untimely death?

Just like with everything else concerning the Civil War, it is difficult to judge the path the US took after the end of the war. The Reconstruction era is regarded to have helped the country depolarize after the Civil War. Many of the policies and legislation introduced during this time reintegrated the South back into the Union. Congress tried to justly approach the problem of racial inequality with the Fourteenth and Fifteenth Amendments, but discrimination persisted for nearly a century, and many argue that it still continues today. The years from the end of the Reconstruction to the 1960s are often seen as one of the most shameful periods in US history.

In conclusion, the American Civil War was a conflict rooted not just in political differences between the Northern and Southern states but also in the different cultures and societal structures of the two sides. The country disintegrated into the bloodiest war in its history while the rest of the world was going through the process of modernization and rapid industrialization. In the end, the North, led by President Abraham Lincoln, triumphed. However, the Civil War's ultimate victory would be achieved about a hundred years later with the triumph of the civil rights movement.

Here's another book by Enthralling History that you might like

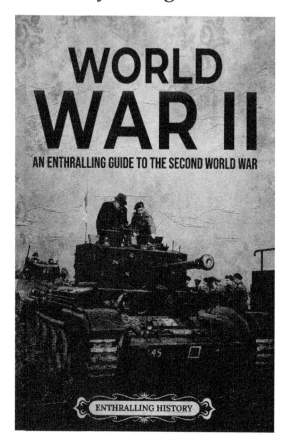

Free limited time bonus

Stop for a moment. We have a free bonus set up for you. The problem is this: we forget 90% of everything that we read after 7 days. Crazy fact, right? Here's the solution: we've created a printable, 1-page pdf summary for this book that you're reading now. All you have to do to get your free pdf summary is to go to the following website: **https://livetolearn.lpages.co/enthrallinghistory/**

Once you do, it will be intuitive. Enjoy, and thank you!

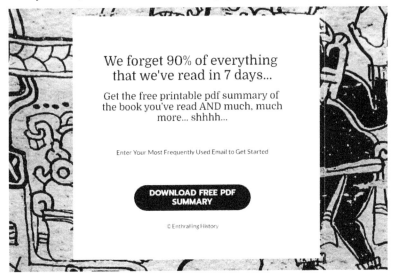

References

1. Arnold, J. R., & Wiener, R. (2011). *American Civil War: The Essential Reference Guide*. ABC-CLIO.

2. Cleland, R. G. (1916). "Jefferson Davis and the Confederate Congress." *The Southwestern Historical Quarterly, 19* (3), 213-231. http://www.jstor.org/stable/30237274.

3. Collier, P., & Hoeffler, A. (1998). "On Economic Causes of Civil War." *Oxford Economic Papers, 50* (4), 563-573. http://www.jstor.org/stable/3488674.

4. Gallagher, C. (2007). "When Did the Confederate States of America Free the Slaves?" *Representations, 98* (1), 53-61. https://doi.org/10.1525/rep.2007.98.1.53.

5. Gienapp, W. E. (1992). "Abraham Lincoln and the Border States." *Journal of the Abraham Lincoln Association, 13*, 13-46. http://www.jstor.org/stable/20148882.

6. Gunderson, G. (1974). "The Origin of the American Civil War." *The Journal of Economic History, 34* (4), 915-950. http://www.jstor.org/stable/2116615.

7. Hassler, W. W. and Weber, Jennifer L. (2022, April 20). *American Civil War. Encyclopedia Britannica.* https://www.britannica.com/event/American-Civil-War.

8. Horwitz, J., & Anderson, C. (2009). "THE CIVIL WAR AND RECONSTRUCTION." In *Guns, Democracy, and the Insurrectionist Idea* (pp. 118-136). University of Michigan Press. https://doi.org/10.2307/j.ctv3znzcm.9.

9. Kingseed, C. C. (2004). *The American Civil War* (Ser. Greenwood guides to historic events, 1500-1900). Greenwood Press.

10. Krug, M. M. (1973). "Lincoln, the Republican Party, and the Emancipation Proclamation." *The History Teacher, 7*(1), 48-61. https://doi.org/10.2307/491202.

11. Peck, G. A. (2007). "Abraham Lincoln and the Triumph of an Antislavery Nationalism." *Journal of the Abraham Lincoln Association, 28*(2), 1-27. http://www.jstor.org/stable/20149114.

12. Reynolds, D. E. (1970). "Union Strategy in Arkansas during the Vicksburg Campaign." *The Arkansas Historical Quarterly, 29*(1), 20-38. https://doi.org/10.2307/40030703.

13. SHEEHAN-DEAN, A. (2011). "The Long Civil War: A Historiography of the Consequences of the Civil War." *The Virginia Magazine of History and Biography, 119*(2), 106-153. http://www.jstor.org/stable/41310737.

14. Sickles, J. (2007). "THE CAPTURE OF JEFFERSON DAVIS." *Military Images, 28*(6), 4-19. http://www.jstor.org/stable/44034528.

15. Surdam, D. G. (1996). "Northern Naval Superiority and the Economics of the American Civil War." *The Journal of Economic History, 56*(2), 473-475. http://www.jstor.org/stable/2123979.

16. Wallenfeldt, J. H. (2012). "The American Civil War and Reconstruction: 1850 to 1890 (1st ed., Ser. Documenting America: The Primary Source Documents of a Nation, vol. 1). Britannica Educational Pub. in association with Rosen Educational Services.

17. Welling, J. C. (1880). "The Emancipation Proclamation." *The North American Review, 130*(279), 163-185. http://www.jstor.org/stable/25100834.

Printed in Great Britain
by Amazon

38465718R00086